designing worship teams

designing worship teams

CATHY TOWNLEY

ABINGDON PRESS / Nashville

DESIGNING WORSHIP TEAMS

Library of Congress Cataloging-in-Publication Data

Townley, Cathy, 1949-
    Designing worship teams / Cathy Townley.
        p. cm.
    ISBN 0-687-09265-5 (pbk. : alk. paper)
    1. Public worship. 2. Church group work. I. Title.
    BV15 .T677 2002
    264—dc21

                                        2002007383

02 03 04 05 06 07 08 09 10 11—10 9 8 7 6 5 4 3 2 1

MANUFACTURED IN THE UNITED STATES OF AMERICA

For my mom, whose ability to create an elaborate and delectable repast from basic ingredients taught me how to organize and develop an artistic experience that might feed a soul; and for my dad, whose entrepreneurial spirit taught me to translate art and design into leadership. Little did they know the ways in which God would use their gifts.

contents

DESIGNING TEAMS

THE DRAMA OF BIRTHING TWENTY-FIRST-CENTURY WORSHIP DESIGNERS

foreword

*T*he most significant change in Christian worship is the shift in emphasis from worship *design* to worship *designers* as the crux of authentic worship *experience*. Today the challenge is not to create "good worship," but to birth "credible, spiritual worship teams." If you dare to read this book to the end, you will not only understand this shift, but you will experience simultaneous stress and excitement as the implications begin to sift into your attitude toward, and planning for, worship with the Body of Christ.

In the old world (through the mid-1970s), church leaders ignored demographic contextuality, constructed liturgies using timeless templates, and recruited professionals to implement the order of service with the highest standards of performance in the denomination.

In the transitional world (from the mid-1970s through the close of the 1990s), church leaders targeted demographic tribes, customized public worship using indigenous forms, and recruited talented amateurs to implement the contemporary order of service with the highest standards of performance in the community.

In the new world that Cathy Townley perceives so well (emerging in the 1990s and stretching into the twenty-first century), the planning process itself has been turned upside down. Instead of identifying a target, planning a program, and recruiting task groups to implement it, church leaders in this new world are first birthing a team, then defining boundaries for their limitless imaginations, and ultimately turning them loose to target, design, and implement whatever the Holy Spirit elicits from their spiritual growth.

The real key to authentic, powerful, useful worship—the kind of worship for which busy people make time to return day after day and week after week—is not really about a good program but about credible people. It is not about a profound preacher, but about a creative team. It is not about a liturgical journey, but about a shared spiritual life. The implications of this shift will make many seminary-trained pastors' hair stand on end, and cause many traditional denominational officials to break into a cold sweat.

Suddenly, the priority of deploying certified clergy who spend all that time researching, rehearsing, and expositing texts from a common lectionary is revealed to be vastly overrated. Church leaders need to birth, nurture, and liberate teams of passionate, missionally focused, spiritually growing amateurs who will replace them as the primary communicators and interpreters of the living Word.

Suddenly, the priorities of customizing timeless, sacramental liturgies to be politically correct and dogmatically pure, gender respectful and doctrinally conforming are revealed as missing the real target of relevance. Church leaders must coach teams in a soul synthesis that merges subjectivity and objectivity and connects God's *kairos* and the public's chaos through the medium of team spirit.

The trouble is that no seminary has trained leaders in these skills, and no denominational judicatory has certified this calling.

This book is for an entirely new generation of church leaders who are creating a new kind of worship experience.

No amount of tinkering with the age-old, modern worship-planning process that moves from principle to program to implementation recruitment will work. It doesn't matter how upbeat the music is, how informal the service becomes, how cute the children's story feels, how cleverly the sermon is delivered, or how inclusively the terminology is customized. The process itself is flawed, and until that process is reversed, worship participation in Christian churches will continue to decline. Begin with people, not principles. Birth a credible team, not a predictable program. Give boundaries, not liturgies. Trust the spirit, not the institution. Christian worship in this *new world* depends less on liturgical blueprint, and more on the credibility, creativity, and coachability of the worship team.

Everybody believes that the purpose of worship is to glorify God. The issue is how best this can be accomplished. Is God best glorified by skillful experts replicating liturgical blueprints for the internal satisfaction of institutional members? Or is God best glorified by spiritually growing teams creating unique opportunities of grace, which will motivate the spiritually hungry public to follow Jesus into the postmodern mission field? If you answer yes to the first question, return this book immediately and get your money back. If you answer yes to the second question, read on, and then pass the book to your best friend.

Thomas G. Bandy
November 2001

designing teams

_____ *setting the stage*

THE DRAMA OF WORSHIP

All my life I've been involved in the arts. I studied music from the age of seven, and dance from the age of five. I was in every play imaginable in high school, and in college at Northwestern University, I was involved in the Waa-Mu Show and Gilbert and Sullivan Guild. My dream was to make my way to Broadway. But the performer's lifestyle would have been my undoing. Instead, God took my passion for the arts into the church, and for that I'm forever grateful.

The arts have influenced the way I see every part of my life, including worship. Worship is drama. Not only is worship a place where the arts flourish, it's a rich story of lives intertwined. There's intrigue, plot, crisis, denouement, and character development. It's about lives—yours and mine—coming face-to-face with a power far greater than we can imagine. It's about the emotional reaction inside a human spirit that realizes eternity. It's about fear and hope, suffering and relief, rejection and acceptance. It's about peace, and love, and being *in* love, and unrequited love; God who adores us and we who want no part of it. It's about reconciliation; reuniting with our first love, our maker. It's about never turning back once the stage has been set and the "performance" light is turned on. It's about ultimate destiny.

When worship is able to find the point of connection between God and human, it recognizes that much has gone before and much is yet to come. Oceans of time and incredible life-changing experiences are expressed in each moment of contact. Worship designers understand that. They search for signs of the drama being portrayed in the lives around them, and they seek ways to let the drama unfold in the time and place called public worship. Worship involves many diverse forms of expression, and in every one of them—no matter what the form—is the potential of witnessing a life changed by the love of God. There is no play or story that is more dramatic than that.

SUSAN SAYS, "LET'S TALK . . ."

DIRECTOR'S NOTES

Susan is a little of me, a little of dear friends and fearsome foes, and a little of you. She is "everyperson" who struggles with life, and whom God adores. Play her with tenderness.

SUSAN

Hi, I'm Susan. I'm nineteen. I just dyed my hair back to my normal color—well, mostly normal. I don't know if you can see the purple and blue streaks. You probably think I look strange. Or, maybe not.

Can I tell you a little about my life? It's important to tell you so that you can understand what has happened.

This is the Reader's Digest version, okay? I dropped out of high school when I was fifteen, and I was so pissed off and mean to

17

everyone that my mom kicked me out when I was sixteen. Well, I was high all the time, and I just hung out and got into trouble. I suppose she needed to kick me out, 'cause I have two younger brothers. Bad influence.

Of course my mom hasn't really been all that great of an influence either. She's kind of screwed up, with relationships, you know? Like I'm not. Anyway, my mom's relationships, especially with men, do not really, like, paint the whole picture. Even though she's forty and has never been married, and my two younger brothers each have different fathers from each other and from me, career-wise my mom actually does okay. She works out of the house, and she makes pretty good money between her Web business and waiting tables. She used to drink a lot, sometimes really a lot, but she cleaned all that up. She's actually a pretty good mom to my brothers now, and she can pay the bills.

I must say, I've definitely seen the dark side of life. I've stolen, I've turned tricks, I've done jail time. I'm actually an addict. I'm in recovery. The hard stuff, not just a little booze like my mom did.

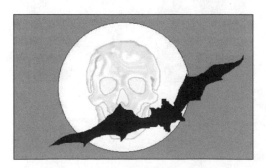

When I was using, I was really attracted to goth and Satanism. Scary. I much prefer recovery as a way to—understanding life. It's not so mean. I'm not so mean. I think that maybe my mom might like me better now too. I'm hoping we might be able to negotiate my living at home again. That's a scary thought. Maybe it might work. We've both changed.

So, now you know where I've been. Like I said, it's important to understand all that so that you can understand this thing that happened.

For about the past month, I've been going to a new NA meeting—Narcotics Anonymous, that is—at this church. I want you to know I've never been anywhere near a church in my life. Church people seem so judgmental. Besides, my mom doesn't go to church. Anyway, my sponsor in NA goes to this church and they had meetings at a better time for my hours, so I started going to meetings there. So one night on the way out, my sponsor Chynna was walking me out while we talked about the meeting and stuff, and we walked past this wall.

Have you ever seen stained glass? Well this wall had these banners with these incredible pictures hanging from it with a light shining down on them, and it made them look like stained glass. Every time I went there I could hardly take my eyes off them. They're, like, vivid! So I thought I'd ask Chynna if she knew what the pictures were all about.

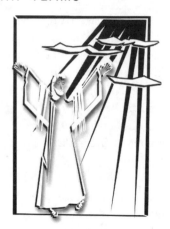

"Yeah. This one," she said, "is the Madonna and her baby—she's the mother of Jesus, who is the Son of God."

I thought, "God had a son? Did I know that? And God's son had a mother who was a human?" It seems like I knew that, but I'm not sure. Wow! 'Cause even if I did know it, it was like I was hearing it for the first time. Did that make God the father then? Isn't God like a spirit of some kind? So then God the spirit had a son with a human woman? Is that possible? This all went through my head in about three seconds. But that picture, you know? I kept looking at it, 'cause what was so strong about it is that this Madonna was totally loving her baby. I kept thinking, "I wonder if my mom ever held me that way."

Well then I asked Chynna about that one with the guy on a cross. I mean, I was wearing earrings that were that shape, without the guy on them. So who is it? "That's Jesus," she said.

"Jesus? The same one in that other picture, the baby?"

"Yes, the same one."

She told me that he was killed by the humans of his day because they didn't believe that he was God's son. Now did you know that? People killed him because they thought he was a fake! I couldn't believe I never heard that before. The feeling inside me was— like—well it was like the way I felt when I realized my mom was kicking me out. I mean, it really, like, punched me in my gut to hear that.

I just kept looking at that picture of him on that cross. He had holes in his feet and hands, with nails through them. God, how awful. God must have felt so terrible about that. The Madonna too—Mary. But you know what the weird thing is? I have holes too. In this really strange way, it was like I could relate. I kept thinking that he had a lot of holes, but that I thought maybe I had more. All my studs and rings. And then when I used to shoot up, you know. The holes are kind of all over me. I don't know. Is it fair to wonder that?

So then I asked Chynna about that picture that looked like a big circle. It had a picture of Jesus' face on it, but the picture was faded, like it was symbolically in the middle of the circle, or even behind it. Chynna told me the circle represented the stone that was in front of the tomb they buried Jesus in after he died. God's son died. He was in that tomb for three whole days. Speaking of being able to relate. Do you know how many empty "tombs" I've slept in over the past couple years? Really dark and cold. And lonely. So that's what happened to Jesus. Isn't that incredible to you? When I looked at the picture again, I could see that the cross he was hanging on was now broken apart—like, shattered. Wow!

And then in that last picture. Jesus was kind of in the air. Now this will freak you: Chynna told me that Jesus escaped from his tomb of death! He died, and then he came back to life, or like Chynna said, he rose from the dead. Just flew away. I mean, that is so hard to believe. Except that, in a way, I have also kind of risen from the dead. There have been many times. . . . Well, I won't go there right now. But I know it's possible in some way. But I'm not really dead, like he was. So this is different too.

I must have had this really stunned look on my face or something, because Chynna said, "Susan, you and I—we've seen the dark side of life. So has Jesus. And I know you know that, just by looking at you. Now I want you to know, for me, that's really important. I don't think I could relate to a higher power that didn't know what it meant to suffer. Jesus does. And look, Susan. Look at that picture. Jesus rose from his suffering, and that means you and I can too. That means we can be free of our wounds too. We don't have to prove anything; we don't have to stay locked in a cycle we

21

can't get out of. We can actually have joy and hope in our lives in spite of everything we've been through. That's the kind of lasting love he has to offer."

You know, life is really a struggle. I mean, recovery has been really cool for me. I need it. But this is, like, so deep. I mean, I just kept staring at those pictures. Chynna is so cool. She just waited. . . .

BE AFRAID, BE VERY AFRAID

DIRECTOR'S NOTES

Playwrights write because they feel they have something to say. What they have to say about their topic is often both cynical and optimistic. So too with this book; there is a motivation for having written the words and ideas in the following chapters, and that motivation is shared in the next few pages. What you will read there offers both the foundation for criticism and hope for the future that have been building in me for some time.

In the past year, I've had a disturbing awakening that has left me feeling worried. I've discovered that there are many church leaders who don't seem to be aware of or care about transforming one's soul in Jesus Christ.

Though training events are filled to the max with participants who want to learn about reaching people in the new millennium, the unspoken agenda is the desire for cookie-cutter solutions. People want formulas for growth and change, particularly in the area of worship design, and many trainers and speakers are trying to give them those solutions. The formulas will give church leaders the bigger church, help them compete in the church marketplace, and ease their tension over why they don't seem to be drawing people from the community into the local church.

But transformation of the soul because of a relationship with Jesus is not about formulas or technique. It's an ever unfolding drama of heart, faith, journey, time, space, and all the intangibles that define one's relationship with the Holy, and it must be experienced; it can't be reproduced. Understanding that must be the basis of worship and worship planning, because it changes your view entirely about how to develop worship in a world that is so fundamentally different than ever before. In today's world, more than ever, cookie-cutter solutions and formulas lead one on the road to failure, and serve as a handy deterrent, preventing one from going as deep as a person can go with Jesus.

Whenever I ask church leaders why they want to start a new worship service, I typically get one of three answers: pressure from a higher source like a denominational official; a desire to increase numbers and "keep up with the church Joneses"; or pressure from within the congregation to present a different style of music. Rarely do I hear from church leaders what I personally long to hear: that they want to start a new worship service because they live to share the love of Jesus with the world, and this new worship service is the best way they can think of to fulfill their dream.

That's passion—and passion is what you need to start a worship service. But passion is something you can't package. It has to be real and emerge from a deep devotion to loving God with every fiber of your being. Why don't church leaders have more of that? Is it because passion has become taboo in the modern era? Is it because they never had it, or have forgotten it? Is it because church leaders don't really know Jesus? Is it some combination of these or other factors?

I'm not sure. But one thing I've noticed is that many church leaders seem to have their heads in the sand about the chaos of the changing world. It would be very nice to get an easy formula for starting a new worship service so that you don't have to face the incredible unfolding drama of life in the new millennium. Church leaders want formulas, and postmodern people run from formulas. I'd call that a "disconnect."

In *postmodernity*, values, style, culture, learning, technology, attitude—everything is different from the *modern era*. If church leaders want to start a worship service in today's world, it will involve paying close attention to postmodernity, and it will involve careful and close personal self-examination. The question to ask oneself is, "Who is Jesus in my life, and how can I share my experience of him with others?" That's where this journey must begin, because answering that question opens the door to clarity and focus, and also prepares you internally to be able to accept change. If you are so in love with Jesus that you will do anything so that others can know him, then watching, understanding, and adapting to cultural changes isn't that threatening, even though the culture is so frighteningly different.

I say "frighteningly," because change is not easy for anyone. The truth of the emerging culture in our brave new world is that Christianity is moving out of the institutional church. That's difficult for church leaders to grasp. But understanding this one point is essential to being able to make the shift from modernity to postmodernity. Young people who haven't known Jesus before, and who are now finding Jesus and changing their lives because of Jesus, are often filled with disdain toward the mechanical, formulaic church that cares only for its own preservation. They want no part of an institution that values solutions over passion. And those are the ones who *are* finding Jesus (miracle of all miracles), because much of America is finding other pathways to the truth, of which there are many.

Diverse populations in America today have no real understanding of Jesus—a phenomenon that is becoming more prevalent as we move deeper into the twenty-first century. It's as though they've never really heard of him. They can't tell you the story of his life, or what it means to have a relationship with him; or they've heard of and have no interest in the institutional Jesus, who's so ancient that he doesn't speak to the needs of real people; or they find him bland—an irrelevant dogmatic who can't communicate to a changing world, but who thinks he's right and everyone else can go to - - - -.

That's the influence of the "club." In the Christian Club (AKA "the *Christendom* church"), members won't give up anything that threatens their own status quo. The ethos of the club is manifested in the concern over preserving the institution before including non-Christians in the kingdom of God; the former keeps things the same, and the latter means change. The Christian Club thinks that the dominant worldview is Christian, and everyone, therefore, innately understands the rules of the institution. So why fix it if it ain't broke? Seeing the world that way is the safety net for Christendom. If the Christian Club believes that everyone knows Jesus and, therefore, they also know the institution's rules, Christendom doesn't have to deal with postmodernity.

Will the real Jesus please stand up? One of my favorite books, *The Sacred Romance* (Brent Curtis and John Eldredge [Nashville: Thomas Nelson, 2001]), dares to talk about our relationship with God as a wild romance, in which God is our jealous lover, coming after us at all cost and asking us to reject our other lovers like pride, low self-esteem, busyness (or the mechanical formulas of the church?), or even a physical lover. We all have lovers that seek to take us from God, and affairs and addictions are only symptoms of the deeper wounds that cause us to take a lover in the first place. We give our lives to such lovers, real or metaphorical because we seek anything to keep us from the intimacy of a true lover's relationship. God offers Jesus the romancer, the greatest source of intimacy for any human. God continuously offers Jesus to us, desiring us to receive and live for his passionate love.

Intimacy, by definition, breeds change. It causes one to act and interact to the deepest place of one's being when becoming truly intimate with God or another human being; therefore, you don't remain the same. That's the opposite of Christendom. Church leaders and churched people flock to mechanical formulas for success in their parishes as a way to avoid facing the drama of a life with Jesus, which is the essence of change. But then, I speak from experience. In my whole adult life, I have tiptoed around the edges of such depth with Jesus, never really going to the farthest reaches of where he could take me—until recently.

This Jesus is the one who stands as real among all imitators;

the passionate wild romancer, who is both cosmic and contextual; and who I believe can change the lives of twenty-first-century people. He is neither moralistic nor morose; not lifeless or remote; not formula or fiction. He is the incarnation, the real-life flesh and blood of God. No other world religion or alternate spirituality can boast that claim; only Christianity has God in the flesh, the living God. Jesus is the true source of human transformation. Doesn't that warm your heart and stimulate your soul just a little?

The new culture doesn't frighten me at all; in fact, I believe it's our friend and can help us reach a world drastically in need of a savior. I'm only frightened when we would put our comfortable solutions before the risk of following Jesus, no matter where he leads us, even into the world.

For worship designers, comfortable solutions and formulas often include words or catchphrases like "music," "thematic dramas," "style of worship," "multisensory," "multimedia," "experience," targeting Boomers, Gen-X, and Millennials. As important as all of that is, it's not what worship is about. Worship design is about the drama of lives changed through the journey of faith, and it's about developing people who dream visions of portraying God's faith in the world through worship. That's the part you were born to play; to focus on anything less is mere illusion.

reading through the playbook

HOW TO WRESTLE WITH THIS OCTOPUS

A playbook is for directors, actors, crews, and students of the-ater. It contains not only the script, but also notes that the audience never sees, but which help give insight into the drama. The audience ultimately experiences those insights when the drama comes to life upon the stage. This particular "playbook" has no script, but it is a collection of ideas to provide a glimpse into your role as a twenty-first-century worship designer, which ultimately involves the congregation and community in the midst of which you serve Christ. The next chapter resembles a scene description of the various components of the drama.

Worship isn't simple. As a drama, it's a deep experience, and deep experiences are never simple. Therefore, worship *design* isn't simple; it can't be, if it's to speak to the true nature of what happens when human and God interact, which, by definition, is worship. Indeed, worship design is complex, unpredictable, and irrational, centering on an ever evolving plotline of God and human seeking each other. Many who read this book will find it a challenge because it reflects the chaos of worship design. However, worship design evolves, as does a human life, with God in it. Therefore, there are no timelines to help determine the next step for developing a new service or a team; no clear examples of worship design from an existing, successful service that seems to reach people in the new millennium; nothing to "simplify" planning and leading. There's no script.

> We're often tempted to see the threads of similarity between worship experiences so that we can make our jobs as designers of worship a little easier, but the greater opportunity is in seeing the differences that come from developing the people who develop the worship.

Truthfully, the approach this book takes will make worship design more difficult. When you're working with people to plan and lead worship by growing them as planners and leaders, you're working with them in the most profound capacity possible, since worship is about faith development. Just as great directors help actors dig inside their own resources and experiences to ultimately understand and portray their characters, the growers of worship designers must coach and mentor them to grapple with their own faith journeys, as well as to speak with the faith journeys of others. That doesn't happen in a straight line.

Further, we're smack-dab in the middle of postmodernity, and communication has changed. Technology has influenced learning, values, lifestyle, and much more. Life itself has become irrational and chaotic. Like a powerful drama that has verisimilitude, twenty-first-century worship and worship design will reflect the nuanced, layered, optional, intuitive, and nonlinear ways in which people think and live today.

And perhaps most important, the nature of worship is simply unpredictable because it involves the Supernatural, and that makes worship design something you can't package. Every drama is different, for every life is different, and therefore every actor brings something unique to the role; every worship team is different, and every worship environment is different. Jesus works dynamically in people, and that's what's important to capture. You can't do that with timelines, solutions, or sample liturgies. And that should be great news to the local church, because getting at the dynamics of a relationship with Jesus is what will reach hearts and souls in the new millennium. You already have the resource to do that; God is already in your midst.

Though this book will feel more cumbersome than other books about worship (which give formulas and solutions), the approach is more accessible than others because you don't have to be something you're not. Many churches believe that to start a new worship service or renew an existing one, they have to be the next Willow Creek. But if worship design revolves around faith, there are many options for beginning your mission that allow for evolution, and still enable you to begin designing meaningful, engaging worship on a very small scale. The focus is on people, and people can do amazing things when there is faith. That is, God can do amazing things through them. All the world is God's stage.

SCENE DESCRIPTION

The worship designer can read through the drama in any number of ways. It doesn't matter if you choose to read through one page after the next, or if you'd rather follow the threads represented by each category described below, or if you'd rather design your own approach. The process you choose is part of the experience of reading for the part.

Enter worship designer; enter with heart.

Who is the worship designer? It is everyone who worships. Each designs worship in daily interaction with God in their own lives, and in public worship in the presence of others.

Setting the Stage (*The Drama of Worship*): At the very beginning of the book, you'll learn a little about me and get a taste for why it's helpful to see worship as drama.

Reading Through the Playbook (*How to Wrestle with This Octopus*): You are here. Feel the part.

Going Behind the Scenes (*Up with [Postmodern] People*): A great drama takes place not only on the stage, but also in the many months of rehearsal prior to performance, as actors work to understand the driving force behind the characters they portray. The next chapter sets the stage for worship designers as they prepare to enter into the drama of worship design. In it, I will discuss the "why," "how," and "what" of teams and their importance for twenty-first-century worship design.

The Plot (*Six Characteristics of Great Worship Teams*): At the beginning of this section I have included a synopsis of the entire book. Read it before you read Act 1 so that you will understand the story line and what ties all the players—the vast array of worshipers—together. In a sense, the drama you're about to enter is a play within a play, within a play. There's a cast of characters (Susan, Jeremy, etc.) who tell one story; then there is you and the story you have to tell; then there are all the others whom you represent and all their stories. If you read the drama with only one story in mind, you will have missed the many intricate living connections where God is at work. Reading the plot will help put a prism before your eyes.

Acts 1-6 (*see Contents for individual titles*): There are six worship principles for you to study, understand, and teach your team. The principles will help you focus on the team instead of the worship service per se; the team will then focus on the worship service. By focusing on principles for developing teams instead of teaching Method acting, your team and the worship itself will be more able to adapt to the changing culture.

The Cast: In the beginning of this book, the character Susan was introduced. She has several friends and acquaintances. Read their stories at the beginning of each act. See the cast list and a brief character description below.

Character Development: Great actors are masters of self-examination; they dig into themselves to find the resources to portray a part authentically. In most of the chapters of this book, you'll find the subtitle "character development"; the bulleted headings that follow are topics that represent the "glue" for forming teams—concepts or suggestions that will help you go deeper within yourself, with God, and with each other.

Stage Directions: At the end of each chapter are ideas for growing your team. Stage directions include simple ideas for team development; feel free to expand upon or change them. There's also a section called "If you're starting a new worship service," which is geared to those using this book to launch a new team-based service.

Scene Connections: To help you gain deeper insight into the connections between different parts of the book or story line, there are "hyperlink" buttons that will allow you to fast-forward or return to information related to your current topic.

Asides: Actors sometimes break from the scene they're in to speak directly to the audience about a topic related to—but not identical to—the scene from which they're breaking. This technique is called an "aside." In every act of this drama are asides or "inset boxes" that have stories and insights from my own experiences as a worship designer that enhance the topic of the chapter you're currently reading.

Entr'acte: You may need to take intermissions from this book to do related research. (Great actors always live their parts both on and off the stage.) Check out the following:

<www.wellsprings.org>—teaching and resources (Don't miss the visual arts page. There you'll find numerous art sites.)

<www.easumbandy.com>—many resources for teaching and networking.

<www.link2lead.com>—demographics, psychographics, leadership.

<www.barna.org>—cultural trends from an evangelical perspective.

<www.christianitytoday.com>—leadership.

<www.rockinauburn.com>—go to "helps for church planters," then go to "Web sites." You'll find art and teaching sites to peruse.

<www.christusrex.org/www1/vaticano/0-Musei.html>—
Vatican art, art resources.

THE CAST, IN ORDER OF APPEARANCE

Susan:	A nineteen-year-old woman who's searching.
Jeremy:	A young man, midtwenties, who has felt God's power.
Vicki:	A middle-aged mom who has been turned off to religion.
Daniel:	A friend of Vicki's daughter; Daniel is a nonbeliever.
Chynna:	Susan's sponsor; she introduces Susan to Jesus.
Don and Meredith:	The parents of Jeremy's girlfriend, Jennifer. They are middle-aged Christendom people who fear change.
Pastor John:	A Christendom pastor who's biding his time until retirement.

STAGE DIRECTIONS

A desired result of working through this book is the birthing of a team or teams to study and develop worship. Teams tend to evolve out of both need and vision for the future; therefore, it's likely that as you work through the pages of this book, your team configurations will grow. It would be counterproductive to suggest a team structure for you to copy; yet, it may be helpful to consider some of the types of worship design teams that often emerge in many worship arts ministries. Perhaps you'll find that you naturally fall into a team formation that resembles the teams below, which are identified by function. You may also find that God has something else in mind for your ministry.

VARIOUS CREWS

The *Start-Up Team* discerns God's movement in the local church and surrounding community. The main role of this group is to *listen* in order to gain insight into the mission of worship. Out of a clear understanding of mission will come awareness of the type/style of worship the church will offer.[1] Together, members of the Start-Up Team will study demographics and the Bible, break bread together, and pray. The people on this team may or may not stay connected throughout the long-term process of team development. Some of them may become a part of another future worship design team, but others may have a more short-term involvement.

The *Worship Planning Team* plans worship weekly. In the beginning stages of this team, the focus will be mainly on education and establishing relationships through study and prayer. Some who take part in this team will likely be artists; but it isn't necessary that all be artists. It's more important to find people with a passion for worship who think creatively and also see the need for change. This group needs a fairly high commitment from its members, and participants may wish to make a long-term commitment of perhaps a year or two.

The *Worship Leading Team* leads worship weekly. This team may begin with just one person on guitar or keys leading praise and worship and grow to a larger team; or it may begin with more instruments and artists as a part of the team. The "main" worship leader may or may not be a part of the planning team.

The *Stage Crew, Technical Teams, Art and Design Teams*, and other behind-the-scenes groups who work together toward the goal of worship design are sometimes forgotten. There are often profound "disconnects" between artists and technical crews, or between up-front leaders and behind-the-scenes worship de-

---

1. *Waking to God's Dream: Spiritual Leadership and Church Renewal* (Nashville: Abingdon, 1999) by Dick Wills is an excellent book about listening to God. Dick is lead pastor of Christ Church in Ft. Lauderdale, Florida, and a frequent speaker on the topic of spiritual leadership.

signers; but the hand is nothing without the foot. As teams multiply in your church, it's important to remember the foundational ethos of *team*. For example, the Stage Crew and Tech Teams are as much a part of the overall spirit of teams, and must be led as teams and think of themselves as such. Further, artists and up-front and behind-the-scenes worship designers must see themselves as part of the same mission.

I almost hate to suggest a *Prayer Team,* since every team that forms should be immersed in prayer. Yet, it may be important to develop a group of people whose role it is to lead intercessory prayer for various worship teams, in addition to the individual teams praying as a normal part of their activities. Some see it as their role to pray above all else. That's their gift.

Casting the Vision will occur throughout the process of team development. It will take different forms depending on what part of the process you're in. In the beginning phases of forming teams, casting the vision is targeted. Finding the right people for various teams involves sharing your vision with one person at a time and watching whose eyes light up. Eventually, all teams cast the vision as worship designers live out their calling.

As you think of people who would be ideal for these teams and begin to form these individuals into teams, think not only in terms of those who are gifted whom you know in your community, but also of those who are at the fringes of community life. God is working in both places, and he may surprise you with those he is already preparing for the harvest.

———going behind the scenes

UP WITH (POSTMODERN) PEOPLE

What you see on the stage is but a fraction of what it takes to produce a drama; so too with public worship. Behind the scenes of public worship are worship designers; behind the scenes of worship designers are individual lives; in each individual life is a story waiting to be told; and in each story God is waiting to be revealed.

Worship design is an art form. The art is in growing a team of people who are called and gifted to design worship. The specific worship your community offers can't stand in isolation from the people who design it, lead it, or participate in it. Worship design is born from the mix of activity among your team, God, the local church, and the community you serve.

It's difficult to fully articulate what happens when working with teams to plan worship. The team affects the worship, the community affects the team, the worship affects everyone, and God is in the midst of it all. The entire experience is evolutionary and chaotic, and it changes everyone who's involved in it. Have you begun to wonder why you started down this path?

Worship is a community-wide event, and though planners and leaders design it beforehand, it ultimately happens live. All the planning in the world can't lead one to predict what God will do in the moment. God is the ultimate worship designer.

36

WHY TEAMS?

"Plug and chug." I heard that phrase for the first time from my friend who serves as a pastor in California. She was trying to describe the traditional approach to planning traditional worship—a habit she didn't want to develop in her new Sunday night worship. It's the "create a form that has the same order of worship every week and just change the music, readings, and leaders' names" syndrome. *Plug* in the title and *chug* out the service. It's the way churches have operated for years. It makes the job of the worship planner—usually the senior pastor or perhaps even a staff person—seem much easier. In a church in which the senior pastor or other staff member does everything, worship needs to be cranked out lest it bury you.

There are multiple problems with that scenario. First, plug and chug can lead to bore and snore. Fill-in-the-blank worship has huge potential to lose its meaning and become rote and empty. Why use a worship team? Because it's an effective antidote to bore and snore. It's much harder for worship to become stale with ideas floating around from more than one person. Further, the world moves faster today than ever before. In postmodernity, you need a team just to keep abreast of cultural changes so that the communication of the gospel can remain relevant.

> Why teams? Because to *not* use them is to miss an incredible opportunity to reveal God.

The other problems are deeper. In some churches, plug and chug is the ethos of "pastor fetch." It indicates unconscious collusion between the pastor or other leaders and the congregation to have the lead pastor, or the right-hand person, or both do everything, be at all the meetings, and be political. Thus, the thought of taking the time to change your style and work with teams to plan and lead worship is daunting. And new church-start pastors (who often find themselves with at least as many plates spinning as do established church pastors) can be in the same boat. In either case, in order to make the shift into teams, a lot must be relinquished. For example:

Control

Pastors who "fetch" are people pleasers. They make decisions on the basis of pleasing those in the church with the most power. In the process, they manipulate others around them so that they can continue to please. However, teams are autonomous and are beholden only to the mission of the church, not to personal or external desires or control. People-pleasing pastors either have to give up their manipulative tendencies to function in teams, or there is insurmountable conflict between the team and the pastor. If the pastor doesn't change or leave, the team won't survive, because the pastor's control is too powerful.

Other Jobs Besides Worship Planning and Team Development

Team development is a big undertaking, especially if committees organize the church. Some pastors or leaders think it's okay to "hand off" a new worship service to a volunteer or other staff person without addressing the impact of a new team structure on an existing structure. But it isn't effective or moral to do so, since new worship services and teams always cause conflict in an existing system. The shift to teams works best when pastors are able to pull out of "task" responsibilities and begin to devote most of their time to building leaders and changing attitudes so that systemic change can occur.

> Pastors don't always grasp how important worship is for God. Worship is God's milieu. God can ambush the least-suspecting person and change a heart forever in worship. When pastors or church leaders want to throw in a little drama here or a song there and think that's all they need to do to make worship meaningful, it doesn't honor the great potential that exists for God to be God.

The "Lone Ranger" Approach

If a pastor is operating in "plug and chug" mode, he or she is essentially a lone ranger. This approach is designed for efficiency, rather than for developing people. It's a radical shift of energy and time to go from "plug and chug" to team development, and it often seems much easier to pastors and leaders to continue working alone than to change styles, even if the pay-off for changing styles would be huge. The problem is that lone rangers simply cannot keep up with worship that will reach nonbelievers in the twenty-first century. Postmodern-worship designers always operate in teams of some form.

Peace at All Cost

Team development and worship changes mean change for everyone in the system. There is no more conflict avoidance; in fact, in postmodern/organic systems, conflict is embraced as an opportunity for growth. That's a fundamental shift in outlook for most church leaders who think that conflict is either a sin or too upsetting to face.

Spinning plates is an illness when taken to the extreme, or when used as an excuse to avoid change. Ultimately, we spin plates to avoid God, who, when we allow it, always takes us to the deeper place of seeing our resistance to him. What might some of the reasons be that would keep you spinning your plates and thereby prevent you from participating in teams?

THE NEED FOR RECOGNITION

I've struggled with this myself. Many pastors and church leaders are talented. They're often gifted in the arts and have a high degree of creativity. Artists and creative types thrive on the recognition that comes from creating a work of art, be it a worship service, a liturgy, a Bible study, or any other thing that a pastor or a church leader is called to do. However, in order to build teams, even the most talented people have to give up the limelight and their need for personal affirmation in order to put others out in front, so that others' creativity can begin to blossom and God can make a statement through someone else. Leaders must rechannel their creativity, using innovation to focus on the gifts and callings of others.

THE NEED FOR POWER

Some pastors and church leaders need hierarchy; they seek respect and honor and have difficulty being on an even playing field with others. It's hard to maintain a clear pecking order when participating on a team, particularly a worship planning team. Worship designers need to have a certain equality, where all ideas are valid and one isn't better than another just because the person who suggested it has attended seminary or has a degree in music.

THE FEAR OF INTIMACY

Some pastors and church leaders struggle with letting down their guard. They don't want to reveal themselves because they worry about not being able to lead. On the other hand, worship designers reveal much about themselves as they struggle together to see what God is doing through them and in the community so they are better able to express that in worship. They share their worries and frustrations, their pleasures and joys, their hopes and dreams, their energy and apathy. The irony is that this type of revelation often makes leaders stronger, not weaker.

THE FEAR OF CONFLICT

Teams are usually a different way for most churches to operate. A committee structure is not a team structure; it's not usually gift based; it's not focused according to a mission; it's often *mechanical* as opposed to *organic*. True teams are everything a committee isn't, and introducing teams into a traditionally structured organization causes conflict. Also, teams elicit a deeper level of relationship, which often means disharmony within the team. The good news is that the disharmony can lead to true spiritual depth, but it's demanding, and many church leaders don't want to take the time or expose themselves enough to operate in this manner.

STRUGGLING WITH FAITH

Some pastors and church leaders don't believe God desires to do anything through them. They struggle to see the bigger picture or to believe that God has a vision. When there's a dry spell that yields no talent to harvest for the band or worship team, church leaders often feel discouraged and give up. But sometimes, dry spells are God's most fertile time. God may see a need to tweak a direction or change a motivation in you or someone else before it's time to move forward. Team is about faith, after all.

The dramatic tension of teams is that they bring both significant challenge and opportunities for the Holy Spirit to transform lives. Teams can be a means of grace for letting go of all that keeps you from going deeper with God. But it takes truth telling and authenticity. Spiritual growth is built upon self-examination in the presence of Christ. Leaders must model what that means, and share their own struggles when they apply. Truth telling and authenticity among members of the worship team affect worship and help make worship real.

Character Development: Motivation

Great actors think deeply about the "Why?" "Why does my character get angry, right here, right now? Why is my character silent instead of speaking up?" Great worship teams also ponder questions of motivation, and grapple together with the answers. Consider the following questions:

- Do you yet understand the "Why?" of teams? If not, what are the hindrances for you?
- Is worship central in your life? Is it central to your community? Is worship a passion for you? Do you see it as a life-giving "reason for being"?

41

- What are some life-giving worship experiences you've had? What occurred and what were the components that made the experience meaningful?
- How might your team work together to hold one another accountable to the process of understanding and valuing worship individually and as a community?

WHAT IS TEAM ABOUT?

Teams can be defined on two levels. The first is more obvious: teams are groups of people who gather to accomplish a goal or fulfill a mission. The second is subtler, but perhaps more important: teams, especially worship teams, are groups of people that model and lead change.

Change is foundational to the human experience. In the twenty-first century, speed, flux, and change are intrinsic to living life.[1] It's incumbent upon Christian communities to change with the changing world in order to express the timeless truth of Jesus contextually. Teams lead change in the church, because by their nature, they themselves grow and change; they grow the people who are comprised in them and therefore affect the environment in which they exist to serve.

> Humans have a model for teams in the Holy Trinity. We've been created in the image of God, who has always existed in relationship. Team is in our nature.

---

1. In Bill Easum's book, *Leadership on the OtherSide: No Rules, Just Clues* (Nashville: Abingdon, 2000), he compares life in postmodernity to a wormhole. If you watch sci-fi, you know that a wormhole is an unstable environment that can transfer your spaceship, with you in it, across the galaxy to another reality as fast as you can blink your eye. But a wormhole is unstable, and can collapse on you at any time; therefore, while you go through the wormhole, take Jesus, the guide for your journey. The point of Bill's metaphor is that postmodernity is characterized by speed, flux, and change, and leaders need to know the impact of the new millennium on life in the church in order to be able to take people to the promised land.

When a group of people gathers to accomplish a goal or fulfill a mission, they're making a commitment to be more concerned about the mission than individual gain or glory. Everyone gives 110 percent of themselves to the outcome, putting themselves and their gifts and creativity on the line. In the process, the heart becomes exposed.

> Each person of the Trinity has a noted role to play, which ultimately has meaning only because of the roles of the other two persons. The Father is the Father because of the Son; the Son is revealed by the Spirit. In human teams, team participants have special gifts, which have little meaning outside the relatedness to the other gifts of team members. The whole is greater than the sum of the parts.

For teams to operate effectively, it requires building deep relationships that elicit trust; otherwise no one will feel safe exposing his or her deepest thoughts. Relationship building elicits angst. Many things come out of people when they're working together deeply, and much of it isn't all that attractive. There's anger, defensiveness, pride, prejudice, competitiveness, control; it is difficult. These dynamics are especially prevalent on creative-planning teams like worship and the arts perhaps more so than other areas, because artists are wired differently.

Everyone is guilty of personal "sins" on teams, worship or otherwise. They can't be avoided. It's in facing them that we find the greatest chance to develop authentic community. I've heard many stories from worship designers that match experiences I've had, in which leaders have become frustrated with control or personal pettiness from the people they work with. Drama occurs in the form of conflict when it seems like a team member is sabotaging the project; tempers flare. Then someone begins to see his or her own issues and exposes a little of his or her own heart; maybe it's the leader, maybe it's a participant, maybe it's both. God is there now, directing the flow of energy

43

among teammates by encouraging them to go a little deeper; a bond develops because you've gone inside yourself and your own motivations by sharing them with God and another human being.

Little by little, people begin to give up their pride, anger, control, or whatever else has been standing in the way of growth; people work together a little better than before, and lo and behold, the heart and soul of the team begins to show up in the worship experiences that they design. Personal/individual growth means team growth, and team growth has the potential to affect the growth of the entire community.

The process of team is dynamic, not stable. It never really ends. God always has more for you, another ocean to plummet, or another mountaintop to climb, all of which happens in the midst of relationship. The future of the church rests in the ability of leaders to develop teams of people who are free to flow with the Holy Spirit and grow individually and together. It takes faith and love to do that; faith and love empower the ability to see one's own foibles with joy and acceptance, and forgive the foibles of another.

Faith and love are the spiritual focus of teams. They empower not only relationship growth, but also the larger aspects of change—change within the context of the local church and also in the surrounding community, even the world. Church people try to inhibit change in the church, particularly in worship. However, teams do not permit stagnation, since change is in a team's DNA.[2] The collective faithful love of the team is the backbone by which change is not only acceptable, but a fertile blessing.

---

2. The DNA of the worship team is a metaphor for naming and understanding the way God has been interacting with the team. No two communities of faith are exactly alike; it's as though God puts a thumbprint on a particular group, thereby differentiating groups from one another. The DNA of a particular group is like the DNA of a human being. It exists within the group, designed by God, giving the group character, direction, and identity.

Character Development: Central Themes

Plays often revolve around more than one theme, be it love and justice, rejection and revenge, or many other possible combinations. Actors and directors spend time analyzing the literature to discover the themes to add depth to the production. Worship teams also revolve around several key themes:

COVENANT

God's promises to humans are at the center of our relationship with him and with one another, when we live a life of faith. No matter what we do, God delivers; he brings hope, peace, justice, joy—we have only to receive Christ to know all that he has in store for us. Members of high-functioning worship teams remember God's promises in their relationship with one another, and in the worship they live to prepare. Without the constant return to God's covenant, teams will have trouble recovering from the drama of team life. Unresolved conflict will find its way into public worship sooner or later.

PASSION AND COMPASSION

Worship design is an area of passion. It stirs you. When you're working deeply and passionately with others, you often experience a natural grinding of wills, which must be turned to a positive direction. I've found those who angered me most are those who were most like me. Often, they were the ones for whom I had the least compassion. I wanted them to change right now! I discovered that when you have passion, it's hard to be heard without *compassion*. And whatever the team expresses will find its way into public worship.

WORSHIP

It may seem redundant to say that worship is a central theme for worship teams, yet it's so easy for teams to forget that worship is why they're together. Any number of things distract worship teams, be it technique, style, competition, or moodiness. Worship team leaders need to keep reminding themselves and one another that everything that emerges in team life is potentially a pathway to a deeper plane, and that on that deeper plane is a new revelation about and from God, which is cause to worship. And whatever the team remembers will find its way into public worship.

THE INCARNATION

Christian worship revolves around Jesus, the flesh and blood of God—the Incarnation. For worship teams who love to worship God and bring his love to light in worship, seeing him in the flesh in daily life is vocational. The Incarnation has many implications for human beings, and worship teams continue to see more evidence of that as they study life and know God more. And whatever the team knows will find its way into public worship.

WHO LEADS THE TEAM?

Teams build leaders. Who they are and what they do depend on the stage of development the team is in, and on the different callings of those involved.

Team begins with a "founding" leader[3]—someone who has the vision for team, and giftedness to gather a team. In the case of worship design, this might be the lead pastor of a church, or a worship director/minister, or even a nonpaid servant.

If the founding leader isn't the lead pastor, it's important that the lead pastor be certain of both the founding leader's Christian devotion and openness to the mission of the church. In order to develop others in the team, team leaders of any team in the church must be living a life of study and discipline, and exhibit an unquestionable and humble walk of faith with Jesus. Further, the leader must believe in the mission, or leadership

---

3. Sometimes team begins with someone who has a vision (for team-based worship arts ministry), but who is not called or gifted to develop or lead the team. In that case, either the lead pastor needs to lead, or help find someone who is called and gifted to lead and grow the team of worship designers.

will be at odds. All of these things are in addition to specific gifts and calling that make him or her suited to work in a given area.

> Many pastors of Christendom congregations hand off the responsibilities for beginning a new worship service to a gifted volunteer, with negative results. New worship services cause conflict in Christendom churches. To hand off the project to an unsuspecting and inexperienced volunteer creates more tension and often leads to failure. Lead pastors have a big role in starting a new worship service. It's important they understand and learn to play their part.

If the founding leader is a pastor, particularly a lead pastor of a congregation, he or she must determine his or her specific role in the project. Some lead pastors are involved directly in worship planning, others aren't.[4] However, even lead pastors who don't do "hands-on" worship design remain instrumental in helping turn the tide of "rebellion" that usually accompanies worship changes. At some nonprescribed level, worship design is inherent in the role of lead pastor.

If the lead pastor (or any other founding leader, or both) sees his or her "hands-on" involvement in the design team as short term, he or she must begin to find someone to coach who will take on the leadership position. Leaders (or coaches) usually ruminate on the following questions:

- Who is the right person to mentor?
- How long will it take to mentor him or her?

---

4. I've read that Michael Slaughter, lead pastor at Ginghamsburg Church in Tipp City, Ohio, sees worship design as one of his main responsibilities. He and the worship team gather on Wednesday morning and by Friday they have a worship service, complete with original, homemade but professional-quality video and music, and other artistic and creative endeavors. Kim Miller, the worship coordinator, actually leads the team.

- Will he or she become a paid staff person?
- When will I (the lead pastor) exit from the scene?

Those questions can be difficult to answer. Leadership development is not linear; it takes many detours, making answers to burning questions elusive. Sometimes the first-choice candidate for leader isn't as gifted or as clearly called as it may have appeared; or, it may take much more or less time than anyone could have predicted to mentor someone into leadership. Further, sometimes the lead pastor may find that in the process of trying to work himself or herself out of a job, the pastor becomes involved in hands-on worship planning as a vocational call.

When leaders mentor other leaders, it's more helpful to look for signs to see if the one being coached is ready to move to the next level. Answers to the following questions reveal signs of readiness:

- Is Jesus at the center of this person's life?
- Is this person able to articulate his or her faith journey with clarity?
- Is this person able to express his or her faith journey in abstract or artistic ways? (This is an especially important category for worship teams. Leaders of worship teams need not be artists, but they need to be able to communicate with artists, since the greater share of participants in the worship design team typically are artists.)
- Is this person beginning to mentor others in their faith walk and in their concrete and artistic expression of their faith?
- Does this person have a calling to lead?

When a team leader develops another person to take over the team, his or her role as leader is not necessarily done. Often, a coach who develops other leaders will remain the coach of those he or she develops. There may be less one-on-one time spent mentoring, or different configurations of time and logistics, but leaders need other leaders who have more experience and greater vision in their lives to help them continue on their own path of leadership. True leadership is vocational and evolutionary.

The role of the leader is always to develop other leaders. In the very beginning stages of team, people will depend on the founding leader to lead. However, as the leader continues to help people develop their areas of giftedness and passion, and as they, in turn, begin to take on the risks of self-expression, trust within the team will develop. Participants will lead from their areas of strength, be it artistic ability or perhaps a deeper spiritual gift like prayer, faith, or discernment. There is a synergy in high-functioning teams, and you almost can't tell at times who is doing the actual leading because the energy bounces around like a Ping-Pong ball. The team is the leader.

Yet even at the most mature stage of team, someone needs to be the recognized leader. On some level, the lead pastor serves this function. Though the lead pastor may not be directly involved in the worship team, he or she is fully connected by continually articulating the link between worship and discipleship. In addition, he or she coaches the entire congregation to see themselves as part of the team of worship designers.

For the smaller team that plans worship, someone will serve as the primary coach to encourage worship designers along on their journey. No one ever knows when the next leg of the journey will be revealed, or where it will lead; but leaders will be identified by their abilities to recognize it before others would. The leader of the team is attuned and prepared to encourage people to go to another place with God when the moment presents itself. And as with the Israelites, the team may not want to go. There may be murmurs. The team may resist and struggle all the way to the promised land.

In artistic/creative teams, the promised land is always the deeper place of understanding what God is doing in one's personal life and in the life of the community. That's difficult to see, yet it's the basis for the art. It sometimes requires painful self-disclosure, or letting go to see what God is doing. The person who leads the worship design team must also be on this journey. True encouragement of others often happens best when the leader takes the first steps toward self-discovery.

Character Development: Drawing It Out

Directors and actors are a team. Actors become the part they portray, from the inside out; directors see different dimensions of the part the actor plays because they are looking outside in. Various leaders of worship teams have a little "director" in them, and partner with the team to see the role of team from different perspectives. From all vantage points, team leaders are encouragers who draw Jesus out of one another.

ENCOURAGING LEADERSHIP

Leadership development is relational. Leaders see leadership ability in others and pull it out of them. Sometimes the process is one-on-one, as a coach tells a specific team member what he or she thinks this person's contribution is to the team; other times leaders encourage entire communities about their missional role or purpose. Leadership is encouraging.

ENCOURAGING OBSERVATIONS

Sometimes leaders observe the behavior of another and interpret what they see or hear God doing; sometimes they simply express what they've heard God say in prayer. Expressing God's activity models the process of discernment and encourages others to also notice God. That often leads to the awareness of differing views of what God is doing. Through dialogue, insight into godly activity can be clarified and deepened. Observation is encouraging.

ENCOURAGING PRAYER AND DISCERNMENT

Leaders don't rely only on their own interpretation of God's activity. They encourage prayer and discernment among the team, and often spend time with the team in corporate prayer and discernment. When there's conflict, or a need for more clarity, teams that pray, wait, and listen together, allowing God to lead them through the mire. But it takes practice for teams to pray together. Leaders encourage corporate prayer within their own level of comfort, and their trust that God works through teams and deep relationships. Prayer and discernment are encouraging.

ENCOURAGING CLARITY

Sometimes teams get lost. Leaders continually refocus the energy of the team back to the original vision. And by restating the vision, the door is opened to dialogue, which often reshapes the vision. Leaders are open to the dialogue, recognizing that God works through it to further clarify the direction of the team. Clarity is encouraging.

ENCOURAGING INSIGHT

Human beings see more about what God is doing in the lives of others when we focus on what he's doing in our own lives. When we work to grow and deepen spiritually, it gives us a deeper view of those around us; further, we encourage the process in others, who then, in turn, encourage the process in yet another group of people. Living a life of humility, discipline, self-reflection, and faith while asking others to do the same is a holistic, integrated approach to living and mentoring others. Insight is encouraging.

WHO'S ON THE TEAM?

Change and fluidity are the basis of organization for your worship team. Teams implement change; it's in their nature. The worship design team, perhaps more than any other group in the life of the church, has potential to change life. This team's work to make worship relevant keeps its members focused on the art of expressing the connection to the past, present, and future. They're a link between the established and the emerging, the old and the new, the ancient and the future, the dying and the living.

51

Some teams are very large and loosely connected. My teammates are my mentors, the people whose work I study, and the many people who are doing the same things I am, even though we don't meet or interact in person with regularity. In spite of these differences, we have similar values, goals, and messages, and so we're partners. "Team" is just as much a way of looking at your whole ministry, as it is a specific group that organizes to accomplish a mission.

When teams value and organize around change, it leaves out any prescription or formula for representing certain gifts to form an effective team. For one thing, how any team is structured and who's on it depend, in part, upon who's leading it, this person's leadership and artistic style, values, and so on. Further, artists are not the only people who should be considered for a worship design team, though most likely some will be artists. (Sometimes the greatest contributions artists make to worship design are related to their other gifts—like faith, discernment, hospitality, or giving—in addition to their artistic talent.)

It's easier for one to consider the process of forming teams to be open-ended rather than to be locked into certain categories of people, and then to consider how a certain "category" affects dynamics of the team. For example, you may naturally have artists on your team; then again, maybe not, as it all depends upon what God is doing in you and your community. Selecting a team is about discerning God's activity. You can't say unequivocally that without this or that specific gift or type of person represented, your team can't function. The only exception to that is a leader who encourages other leaders.

Discerning the way God helps you design your team is part of the mystery and excitement of it. Teaming is about the ability to draw out the variety of gifts of the people who are a part of your team. Leaders ask, "Who is God already talking to about this and how can I find them?" When the organization of your team is based upon whom God is calling to be a part of it, as opposed to a preconceived format, it's a whole different ball game.

Character Development: Characterization

Actors learn how to portray a character, in part, by watching people in their daily lives and imitating them. They begin to generalize about groups of people, knowing that certain characteristics identify the aged, teens, polished executives, or the homeless. Characterization can also be a helpful technique for worship leaders and teams; understanding what a certain "type" of person would bring to the team helps to grow the team, should God be calling such a person to the work of worship design.

When gathering the worship planning team, it's most important to begin with prayer, asking God to reveal whom he's preparing for the harvest. Ask God to reveal leaders, and then listen and watch. The positive or negative responses from those you've targeted to the ideas God has given you will provide insight into what God is already up to.

MATURE CHRISTIANS

In working with teams, I've found that mature Christians are those who love Jesus, and who also display the fruits of the spirit, live a disciplined life of faith and love, and continually set aside their arrogance and need to control. Mature Christians are open to constant growth and change.

> In a sense, all of us are artists in worship. Worship touches our passion for life and love and gives rise to personal expression.

FRINGE CHRISTIANS

"Baby" Christians who are just getting to know Jesus can be more open to growth than some "mature" Christians I've met. Certain fringe Christians will bring a wealth of resources to your team, and a fresh perspective on the Christian journey in our changing world. Though it's risky, the rewards of mentoring such a person are great, as long as this person is ready to grow with Jesus and begin taking steps toward leading a disciplined life.

THE CALLED AND GIFTED

No fringe or mature Christian is the right fringe or mature Christian for your team unless these individuals are called and gifted to be part of the team. But how do you know? And how do they know? That's part of the messiness of team; putting your team together is a journey of discernment and discovery.

ARTISTS

As an artist, I can say that we're difficult to work with, and it's important to understand our insecurities in order to help us grow as Christians. Though we're able to help people go deep because we've gone deep, we so crave affirmation that when we don't get it, we think we've "mucked up," even if someone else has been so moved by what we've done that he or she is unable to speak. We need accountability and a lot of grace.

LEADERS

Leaders of worship teams are mature Christians who have certain artistic gifts and a calling to lead. Such team members are very accepting of the foibles of their teammates; they lead others by being open to personal confession and self-examination. Leaders often need to ask for forgiveness from the team. That's how other team members learn to do the same thing.

VISIONARIES

Visionaries hear what God is doing and see where God is leading. It's not about my vision, it's about God's. Visionaries also connect godly visions in different people, though each vision may appear to be different from another vision.

PROFESSIONALS AND AMATEURS

Paid professionals can give time and experience to your community. For most churches, the worship arts ministry is a point of entry; the people who land there are typically not professionals in music and the other arts, nor are they always mature Christians or artists. Someone needs to coach them artistically and spiritually. It's helpful to pay someone to do that so this person can devote the necessary energy to the process.

STAGE DIRECTIONS

Need an intermission? Find a mantra. A song or praise chorus can be repeated in your head throughout the day to remind you of your role as vision caster. There's a short song on one of my CDs called "Dream Your Dreams." I've used it in worship as a liturgical response to prayer, as well as a praise chorus at the end of a praise set. I've also used it to encourage myself to remember that my work is about dreaming God's dreams and sharing those dreams with the world.[5]

Another option for remembering your purpose is to carry a symbol with you that can help to trigger your thoughts and feelings toward God and encourage you throughout each day toward his plans. This symbol can be a powerful reminder when you are away from the local church and it can center your thoughts on your specific work in preparing for a new service or a new approach to leading your existing service.

If You're Starting a New Service

Think about visiting some contemporary worship services in your area. As you visit, consider the following questions, or develop a list of your own questions for your team to struggle

---

5. "Dream Your Dreams," Cathy Townley, © WellSprings Unlimited, 2000. The song can be found on the WellSprings CD, which can be ordered through <www.wellsprings.org> or <www.easumbandy.com>.

with. One caveat: your experience in worship and your responses to your study questions aren't the final answer; experiencing other worship is secondary to God's specific call for your team and community.

- When you visit other worship, analyze how you feel, and also observe how other worshipers act and participate. Does it seem as though your feelings match the worshipers' behavior? How do you interpret your response?
- What are the demographics represented in the service? Do you sense that God is calling you to reach a similar or different group?
- How else does this experience begin to shape your identity in terms of what God might be calling you to offer to the community in worship? Or is there even a connection? That is, is God doing something entirely different in you and the team that isn't seen, heard, or known in other worship you've yet experienced?

the plot

SIX CHARACTERISTICS OF GREAT WORSHIP TEAMS

DIRECTOR'S NOTES

Before a play is staged, the actors and their director always read through the script together and talk about the meaning of the play. They must grasp the point before they can bring their characters to life. There is actually a "plot" to this book: the six characteristics that define great worship teams. Grasping the gist of the plot in the next few pages gives context to your role, which you and God will create together, as you go.

Contrary to popular opinion, the drama of postmodern worship isn't about multimedia, multisensory, technology, performance worship, participative worship, or experiential worship—even though worship is precisely about those things since they define our culture and the new generation. But in a world in which communication takes so many forms, it's tempting to focus on style and technique as the first step to planning and leading worship in the new millennium. I'd suggest that's the wrong order.

> When you understand the true nature of "team," you begin to see that the worship leaders and the congregation are a team, since they work together to "execute" worship each time they meet. There are many such configurations. Team is both big and small, both specific and general.

Worship design is a deep and intuitive process that's nearly impossible to describe in just a few words. It begins and ends with people and the dramatic tensions of their lives, while technique and style fit somewhere in between these layers. It's difficult to understand how complex worship planning is if you're used to focusing on style or liturgy first, or if you're used to planning worship by yourself. When designing worship with a team, your focus is first on the lives of the people who make up the team. That's entirely different from considering style first. Instead of thinking only about technique, you're developing a variety of leaders who live and breathe to understand God's activity within a given community, both inside and outside the church facility. God is active in both places.

For the leader who has the vision to start either a new worship service or develop a team to design the new (or existing) service, or both, developing the team is where the true challenge lies. It will likely include teaching about technique, but it doesn't assume one technique is better than any other. Of course, if you believe there's only one way to worship, then you can become as focused on technique by using a team as by not using one. However, if you believe that God has instilled incredible fountains of ability and insight into people before you ever gathered your team, it opens the door for powerful diversity in what you're able to do to share the gospel message in worship.

But more important, the development of the people in the team isn't about their own development as much as it is ultimately about the development of those who aren't in the team. The team's whole reason for being is to understand how God is working already within the community, so that it isn't just a community, but a community of faith. There is the reason for worship: adoring God for what he's doing. For a team to be able to do that, members must be in constant communication with and have an awareness of the people in whose lives God is at work, which is everyone, including themselves.

It is the role of the worship designer to see what God is up to; to serve as a witness to God's activity; and to help others also begin to understand what God would choose to do and reveal inside a human life. The worship designer is like a playwright who writes a drama so true to life that all who see it recognize themselves in it, and realize they've even been participating in the drama the whole time.

> Birthing worship designers is like working with a living canvas. The grower of the worship designer is the one who stretches the canvas, while God holds the palette and puts the brush to the medium. God's dramatic activity is revealed in each brush stroke.

My inclination is to call this approach to planning worship "postmodern," because it values process over product, and unpredictability over prescription. In modernity, it would have been the opposite. However, no matter what day and age we're talking about, following God is and always will be unpredictable. Just as it was with Abraham, the pathway to discovery for postmodern seekers takes them to some terribly irrational, difficult, and even frightening places. And as with Abraham, worship grows out of every discovery, and worship is also the pathway to every discovery.

> Worship designers include worship leaders who serve in front of the congregation, those behind the scenes, those involved in the arts, ushers, greeters, teachers, choirs, and those in the congregation who worship. God uses the entire experience to bring someone into his presence; therefore, attitudes about worship must be infused into leadership of every dimension.

Meaningful, substantive worship can't be prescribed because it occurs within the context of the journey; yet, most of us are tempted to approach worship design as a formula. We look for trends of culture and try to make judgments about what these trends mean in terms of developing worship. This is fine to an extent; however, we often make our insights into truths that we attempt to apply to every situation. Though there are trends in culture, I daresay most of us have limited awareness of those trends. The world is just too big and the trends go far beyond what we think we know. A prescriptive, formulaic approach to worship, therefore, doesn't allow for the nuances that God might be unearthing as he changes lives, or the wide spectrum of ways in which God expresses his activity. It doesn't allow for God to be unique within a given context.

That's why postmodern worship must be about the faith journey of the worship designers who will develop worship that is reflective of the faith journey of the community within their own cultural context. The entire experience occurs there, even the organization of the team. Who is on the team, who trains or develops the team, how the team is structured, and how many teams you have are all contextual questions that require contextual answers:

- Determining who develops the worship designer means focusing on one's leadership ability rather than one's office. Leaders see God at work in the world and have the ability to assemble others who also see God at work in the world; all have the desire to take the walk of faith alongside others, and all love worship.
- Determining who is on the team means orienting one's vision to gifts and calling as opposed to finding someone to fill a slot that represents a specific task. Called and gifted worship designers have the ability to think deeply and creatively, and they also have a commitment to walk the uncertain journey of discovering God's direction.
- How the team is structured is determined by a creative process of finding an organic structure that responds to the gifts, calling, and styles of the people on the team, as opposed to finding the perfect template into which each character can fit.

- Deciding what style of worship to do has nothing to do with copying Holy Successful Mother Church down the road; rather, meaningful worship responds to what God is saying and doing within your own context, through the people on the team and their insight into the world around them.

My hope is that worship designers would see this approach as good news. There isn't one right way to design Christian worship, and that leaves the door open for nearly anything! For worship designers who have felt the "right way" to reach out has been shoved down their throats, there may be a new ray of hope for diversity and innovative expression. Style of worship is primary only inasmuch as it fulfills the mission. However, I do *strongly* believe that the passion to reach a human heart for Jesus is fundamental to meaningful worship; it isn't "anything goes."

DESIGNING TEAMS: A DRAMA IN SIX ACTS

A playwright is someone who develops a story around specific characters. Playwrights are wickedly insightful when it comes to developing characters. Before they ever write a play, they watch people in the supermarket and at the movies, in the mall and strolling in the park. They eavesdrop on casual conversations of ordinary people and mimic language and dialogue in the voices they give to their subjects of the page. Their keen observations of real-life humans lead to a plot that speaks to the drama of life. When actors bring the characters to life, we who watch are able to see ourselves before our own eyes.

Worship designers are like playwrights. They observe people in everyday life to see how God is already at work, and they design worship that reveals what they've seen. When we, the public, come to worship, we meet ourselves, for we are able to relate to the expressions of God who has already been speaking to us. And like a playwright who sees inside herself as much as she sees inside others, worship designers see God in their own lives. And like a playwright who interacts with the characters he creates, and therefore is changed by the characters he creates, interacting with the faith stories of other sojourners also changes worship designers.

> Worship teams are really all teams who are involved in the life of the church, be it a vision board, a staff, cell groups, or other leadership teams. Each team produces worship by virtue of their interaction with God and the stories of faith their journeys engender. Concepts about worship and the ways in which it comes alive must infiltrate the life of all teams, so that worship is equated with the fullness of life.

Great worship teams birth worship designers who understand the principles by which God works in the midst of life, team, and worship. These following six principles don't provide a formula or a script for selecting, implementing, organizing, or developing the team or the worship. However, they do engage the "grower" or "director" and those he or she is nurturing—the playwrights—in digging deeply to discover God's call in their midst, so that they are changed by the work of team and worship design. Worship design has a life of its own.

Act 1: Worship Teams Have Clear DNA

Worship teams know who they are because they can identify what God is doing in their midst; the DNA is unmistakable. DNA is the beginning, middle, and end of God's activity in a person and in a community of faith. DNA is never fully revealed; with God, there's always more. But great worship teams do have a direction in mind, a mission and a vision, values and beliefs that give them a sense of purpose and identity. God continues to fine-tune the genetic code through the process of developing the worship designers. Worship design is a means of grace, and an opportunity for God to grow people who see that God is active in the world and who wish to praise God for his enduring love. Discovering the DNA of the team and community through the vocation of worship design is an ongoing holy experience.

Act 2: Worship Teams Feel the Dynamism of God

It's essential and impossible to articulate God's activity in worship. It's impossible because it's supernatural and filled with surprises. God's power is unpredictable. It's essential because worship designers need to know the ways in which God interacts, so that worship opens doors. And to say that is to immediately underestimate God's activity, because even in worship that seems dull and lifeless, God can work miracles. Still, we don't really want dull, lifeless worship. Articulating what happens when God and human meet in worship is the constant endeavor of the worship designer. It's a task we can never fully accomplish, yet we know it in our souls, in a language that defies words.

Act 3: Worship Teams Watch Cultural Trends

Relevant worship is contextual. Worship always happens within the context of "the journey." Context is culture. The journey is in the "real" world, where God is alive and well, and the twenty-first-century worship designer's role is to help the worshiper see how that's true. But that's not an easy task, since we're in the midst of massive cultural changes. And as we move more deeply into postmodernity, many of us are struggling to be free of "modern" baggage that keeps us from leading our churches into the new era. To make the shift, the culture must be embraced, not rejected. The culture is the tool for knowing and revealing God. Worship designers listen to and watch God in everyday life and know that he is God.

Act 4: Worship Teams Plan and Lead Indigenous Experiences of the Holy

Do you believe that God is already at work within the community in which you are called to serve? Indigenous worship implies asking questions like, "Who is already in our midst that God desires to use to plan and lead worship?" "Who *isn't* in our midst that God desires using to plan and lead worship?" "Who is in or out of our midst who isn't yet worshiping?" "How can we help people connect to what God is already doing in their tribe or community through worship?" Indigenous experiences of the Holy grow out of discovering God's activity in the lives of the worship designers, the lives of the community known as the local church, and the lives of the larger community in which the local church exists to serve God. Everyone who worships— and everyone who will potentially worship—contributes to the contextualization of worship.

Act 5: Worship Teams Are at the Heart of a Larger Organism

Very often, changes begin in churches because leaders decide they want to start a new worship service, or because they're trying to develop a team structure for planning worship. In a Christendom church (either an established church or a brand-new congregation that is organized in a Christendom way), a new worship service or a team structure can threaten the system, since Christendom churches don't easily accept change, and since "team" is the antithesis of "Christendom." Success with any such project will mean systemic change. Attitudes about the importance of worship and team will need to be nurtured. The proper place within the system for the worship design team is at the heart of the larger organism or structure of the church. Worship teams are central to the spirit life of any community of faith; the view toward systemic change will create the place for worship teams within the new organism.

Act 6: Worship Teams Change Life

Change defines worship teams, and in the church, change happens best in the midst of love. To be on a journey with God changes you because of his love, and individuals who design worship should be first and foremost on that journey in their personal and vocational lives. The changes in the lives of worship designers affect worship; worship affects the structure of the church as well as the community of faith; and the community of faith then takes the love of God into the world. Seeing the change that worship teams bring to life brings the worship designer full circle from following the uncertain path of life with God, to discovering God's DNA, to being a part of God's ongoing activity in everyday life.

the drama
of birthing
twenty-first-
century worship

—————————— designers

WORSHIP TEAMS
HAVE CLEAR DNA

DIRECTOR'S NOTES

Actors try to discover the DNA of the character they're portraying. How the character looks, acts, feels, tastes, smells, and sounds—what makes the person tick—make him real to both the actor and, ultimately, to the audience. Worship teams and other bodies of believers also have godly DNA that must be discovered and then articulated, for it is what makes God real in their own lives and others' lives in which God would be revealed.

JEREMY

My buddy Tim was the one who finally got me to come to church. He'd bug me all week at work, and if we'd hang out on the weekend he'd try to convince me I should come with him on Sunday night. Then one day it was September 11. Life is so random. I kept wondering if God was real, since a good God could never let that happen. I guess I wanted to see if God was any better than what I thought, so I finally went to church with Tim.

Tim plays in the band. They're actually really cool. When I first walked in, it was so weird to me to see all these people sitting around talking, when all I could remember from when I was younger was being told to be quiet in church. We never really went very much when I was growing up; my mom and dad got divorced

69

when I was really little and the church kind of shunned my mom. But right away, Tim's church felt different.

When they started the music, it was pretty mellow. Usually it's not very laid-back at all. But that day it was quiet. At one point in the worship, they started burning incense, and they'd light candles, and hit a bell. It was pretty moving.

Last week, I went with my girlfriend to her parent's church. Wow. It was like being in a time warp. That's when I realized how many churches must still be like the one I went to as a kid. I can't see Jen's parents liking what we do at my church. It's partly the way we do things here, and it's partly the way we talk about Jesus that I think would make it hard for Jennifer's parents. In our church, Jesus just will come into your life, no matter how bad it is. So there are a lot of people who find their way to our church who really don't look like people Jennifer's parents would ever accept. In my church, even though lives get changed, and people start to act differently because Jesus is now with them, they don't always look any different from the way they did before.

I see my life being changed. I think about things differently. They always teach us here that everyone is growing, and everyone is learning, and everyone's job in the church is to help others grow. That kind of puts us all on the same page in a way, even though everyone is really in a different place. We all have something to give and something to gain.

I recently met this new woman who just started coming to our worship. She's probably a few years younger than me—I'm twenty-five. She said she writes poetry. It would be cool to have her read some stuff she's written in worship some time. I'd be really interested in hearing about her life. She looks like she's maybe seen some stuff in life already. I wonder how she sees God speaking to her, or if she even sees that yet. Her name is Susan.

Clear DNA is a mystery. To have clarity about DNA, you have to go on a journey, and where that journey takes you is a true mystery that only God the DNA expert can explain.

> I recently heard someone try to help a group of church planters "decide" their DNA. In reality, DNA can't be decided since it already exists and therefore must be discovered.

In a sense, the clarity of a church's DNA is eternally evident; the DNA of the church is our salvation history. The reality of our salvation exists from before God created us, and is continued through the incarnation of God in Jesus. If you're Christian, the connection to God through Jesus is preconscious, and exists in every fiber of your being. It's our identity, and it's what we celebrate each time we gather to worship.

The mission of the church is to connect people with the truth of God in Jesus as it relates to our eternity, that is, our salvation. It's the foundation of discipleship. But I've worried that many church leaders have lost their passion for connecting people to Jesus. I often speculate that if a church had a strong sense of its eternal DNA, it would be so aflame for helping others see and know what it knows, that it would never struggle with worship development and church growth, since the church's behavior and demeanor would be engaging enough.

On the other hand, there are nuances to our salvation that have to do with carrying the message of the gospel to the ends of the earth. When you begin to tell others about Jesus, the door opens widely for all the ways that God works within the context of a human life. Questions about the truth and relevance of the gospel begin to come up, and Christians are called upon to witness. That's where the discussion of DNA begins to take some interesting turns, because a leader also needs to understand culture and communication in order to witness effectively.

Churches and teams are collectively called to the same mission of helping people understand their identity in Christ both eternally and contextually. As with individuals, churches also have differences; each one is unique, and each one has a specific calling in which God asks it to live out the reality of his love. When we talk about gaining clarity about DNA, it's in this arena. The potential for clarity lies in trying to figure out how God intends to use your team and your church to reveal his eternal love contextually, within the community in which you exist to serve.

Unfortunately, when I've heard leaders talk about DNA, clarity sounds like a formula, instead of a journey. We typically articulate the church's DNA in terms of four categories: *values, beliefs, mission,* and *vision.* It's as though some leaders think all they need to do is follow a few simple definitions to write their values and vision statements, then infuse them into the church, so that the church now knows who it is. I believe in God's ability to use anything for good, so I expect that even the "top-down" approach can ultimately have a positive impact.

However, I see missed opportunity for real insight in that approach. What might God be able to reveal if instead of attempting to "power" the process of clarifying DNA, you actually opened yourself up to what may be incredible surprises from God? In fact, the truth about DNA is that it probably isn't ever entirely clear, which may be difficult for us to accept if we're concrete thinkers. You can't go with God and stay where you are; God continues to reveal the truth of our DNA as we develop our ministries. Real clarity about DNA is the knowledge that DNA adapts and mutates over time and through expression. Just when you think you have a handle on it, God reveals more to you; the prescriptive approach doesn't allow as much for that type of godly interaction.

Having clear DNA is a process, more than a finished product. It's an attitude of openness that says that as you grow with God, you change, and as you change, you gain a new understanding of your DNA. It's important to know that each category of your DNA will potentially be altered as God and you work together, but that you can find direction through your articulation of and activity within each category. The irony of that is that you must attempt to articulate what you see God doing, and as soon as you do, you as much as say that, yes, DNA is, in fact, a concrete phenomenon, when it isn't.

So clear DNA is a paradox, and the clarity of it is probably beyond words. The clarity is found between the language that you give to your understanding of God's activity, and the behavior that God's activity elicits in you. Clarity exists in the gaps or layers between living out and simply stating what you see God doing. It involves language, behavior, understanding, communication, and nuance; it's very experiential.

However you express it, an ongoing interest of the worship team is to discover and express their God-given DNA within a community. You may balk at my words if you've already worked with mission or vision, and feel that your community has developed a clear sense of DNA; you may feel that the worship team is supposed to simply respond to what is already in place. In a sense, that's true. The worship team is a part of the larger picture of the DNA of a community, and doesn't really need to develop its own mission, vision, values, and beliefs, although they might do that, since the work is so specialized. In a worship team that typically deals with artists, there may be unique needs that elicit more focused articulation of the community DNA as it applies specifically to the team of worship planners.[1]

> I once saw a special on public television about the origin of life. It stated that the DNA of Africans is far more diverse than that of any other culture, indicating that Africans are more than twice as old as any other culture. I've heard people talk about traveling to Africa, and feeling a connection to the beginning of life while they were there. It's almost as though there's a collective memory that exists inside our genes that connects humans beyond all awareness of time. The church has a genetic code that defines us: our worship and our story of salvation. The memory of that is eternal.

---

1. In one of my worship teams, we reached a point of conflict within the team that necessitated stating our values and mission in the form of a covenant. Some of the values we identified were different from the core values of the church, though they weren't in conflict with them.

But it's true; the worship team doesn't need to reinvent the wheel if the leadership of the community has already been struggling with discovering the DNA. However, as the worship team forms and bonds through absorbing information, vision, call, mission, and so forth, the team still will have an impact on understanding the DNA for the following reasons.

Many—if not most—churches have a committee write their mission statements without ever having paid attention to what God is doing in their midst. The mission seems packaged and empty, because it doesn't capture the nuances of God's involvement. True mission usually flows out of clarity over genetic code. In some churches, the worship team is the first group to explore the idea that there is such a thing as genetic code in a body of believers. As the worship team focuses on and discovers God's values and beliefs within the community, the mission evolves.

But even if the leadership and the larger body have moved beyond rote mission and have been struggling to discover the deeper layers of DNA, the activity of the worship team will influence existing interpretations. It can't help doing so, since worship speaks to history and tradition, to future directions, and to current issues. God's DNA is smack-dab in the middle of the tension between the old and the new, the established and the emerging. For worship to be truly relevant, worship designers must have their ears to the world around them. As a result, they will make many new discoveries that will affect the community understanding and articulation of the DNA.

It's important for worship designers to understand the DNA of the community. They need to understand the different components of a church's DNA as well as how to discover and articulate the genetic code in general since all of that will affect worship, and worship will affect the community understanding of DNA. The drama of birthing the twenty-first-century worship designer has now begun.

Let's take it a step further by coming to terms with what exactly are values, beliefs, vision, and mission. You may have learned some definitions of them already, as I did when I was working in the local church. However, I have personally found that the definitions I learned were too simplistic. Further, we used to talk about mission, vision, and values, but never beliefs. The component of beliefs adds quite a bit of dimension to the process of discovery.[2]

Below are the definitions I have begun to work with:

- *Core values* are the principles by which individuals and communities live, and are observable in daily life and choices. The importance of certain values can change over time, especially as you move through life's journey and experience loss and other life dramas.
- Bedrock *beliefs* are the foundation of how you see God operating in the world. Bedrock beliefs deepen and expand over time.
- *Vision* is the articulation of what you see God trying to accomplish. Sometimes, but not always, visions appear in pictures and are very mystical. You can't fully receive or understand God's vision without also understanding yourself. Vision becomes clearer the more you live it out.
- *Mission* is the pathway to fulfilling what you perceive is God's vision, which in turn is based on an identity composed of values and beliefs.

As you explore the four components of a church's DNA in some depth, keep in mind two things. First, while the order of how you work with your DNA is important in determining how it gets expressed—for example, mission tends to grow out of other parts of the DNA—the process of clarity is actually fairly messy. Discovering one of the four components of the DNA will affect the others, requiring you to revisit the area that you thought you understood, but which now looks entirely different as a result of recent revelations from God. Discussion of DNA

---

2. *Moving Off the Map: A Field Guide to Changing the Congregation,* by Thomas G. Bandy (Nashville: Abingdon, 1998), gives a process for discovering DNA. It's there I learned about beliefs as a component of genetic codes.

looks linear on the page; but in reality, it isn't. Leadership in the twenty-first century simply does not resemble a straight line.

Second, the purpose of understanding spiritual DNA is to see and reveal how God is working contextually, not to follow a formula for stating your community genetic code. There is more than one successful way to enter into this dialogue. However, the process is always pursued both individually and corporately.

VALUES

I find it interesting that there is so much training on the topic of values and DNA for church planters and for those who are starting new worship services, and yet, when church groups meet regularly, the core values that have been established don't always match what people are doing or how they're acting.

Start-up pastors are taught to "discern" God's direction—pray and listen, and name core values. I've wondered if that process is missing something. I value prayer and discernment, but I'm aware that godly understanding doesn't begin and end with my personal relationship with God. God interacts with other people besides me, and therefore, articulating God's values in a body of believers is more complex than simply relying on what God has shown to me alone.

Part of the problem is that church leaders have been taught to believe that they are the visionaries for their community, which means that the vision comes from and through only them.

Genetic code is metaphorical. Almost anything you say about what you value and believe would take you to a deeper place, if you were willing to follow the metaphor to its ultimate conclusion. The language doesn't matter as much as the process; God will use all of it to change you and the community in which you serve, and bring you to the deepest understanding of DNA: God's eternal love in Jesus.

Yet DNA is both discovered and shared, and when DNA revolves around only the pastor and his or her isolated communication with God, DNA winds up neither shared nor discerned, but enforced.

For example, a pastor sometimes has a notion about what the church is supposed to be as opposed to what it really is called to be. This notion filters out in core value statements, but doesn't really reflect the community in which God is active. Perhaps pastors or visionaries want to click with the current generation, so they manufacture values they think will do that, thereby missing God's true intention for this particular body's activity in the world.

If a pastor or leader then decides these values will be the values of the church, one cannot be certain they'll hit the heart of God's activity in the community. Individuals and communities resonate with values that express who they are, which is why core values must bubble up from the bottom, not be disseminated from the top.

I don't know if the fault for obscuring the meaning of values lies with the trainers, with the competitiveness of leaders who want to succeed, or with the human need to make God's activity predictable. Whatever the reason, the depth of meaning for these values has been obscured in recent training that was intended to help church leaders grow their churches. Knowing what you stand for and how God is speaking through the way you live your life is a very deep process that is pursued both individually and corporately. To have core value statements for a church or worship service that are born out of individual pride or an isolated process of discovery misses the power of it all.

Character Development: Motivations

The focus of a previous segment about character development has already addressed "motivation." Motivation is a frequent topic of discussion for actors and directors. In the

77

theater, you can't talk about the "Why?" too much. That's also true for great worship leaders; they grow the "Why?" very large, so that leaders and teams understand their reason for being, and so that other worshipers also know the meaning of worship. Clear DNA speaks to the "Why?" of worship teams. The sections dealing with character development in the rest of this chapter (Act 1) will all be about motivation.

MOTIVATING VALUES

When worship teams go on a journey to discover genetic code and are wrestling to articulate the core values that drive their community, they can come at the process in a number of ways. The process isn't as important as is paying attention to what makes you tick. *Core values identify you.*

WATCH YOURSELF

I once cited excellence as a core value of my ministry; however, I've observed that's not true. I can let perfection go, but I can't seem to walk away from opportunities to help others see how God has gifted them creatively. When someone first taps into God's creativity inside them, the expression isn't always competitive; yet, the expression can speak volumes to another about who God is and what he's doing. Excellence is a great goal, but it doesn't drive me. *Core values engage your passion.*

LISTEN UP

Sometimes we don't hear God quite right. My worship team got angry with me when I first talked about subdividing them to accommodate growth; they valued relationships and thought a new team structure would inhibit intimacy. We soon discovered that God's value was community and that community is different from simple relationships. Community is missional. Our perception of relationships as a core value was close to God's mark, but God had to shape us. *Core values speak to godly visions.*

LOVING AND LOSING

In one's personal life, loss is often the pathway to understanding what you really care about. It took many losses, including the death of a sibling, to show me the importance of my family. That's also true corporately. When communities lose their way, God seeks to redeem them, and take them back to the place where they began, when there was hope and a view for the future. *Core values have deep roots.*

RANDOM ACCESS

In order to find out what God is doing in people's lives, some churches will send listeners to community gathering places—like bars, bakeries, coffee shops and health clubs—to eavesdrop on conversations and get a glimpse of the spiritual yearnings of the public. As listeners try to discern what God is saying through the public's expression of their hopes and dreams, they, in turn, get a sense of what God is calling them as a community of faith to speak to with their various ministries and worship offerings. What's interesting is that different observers from different communities of faith could do the same project within the same area, and each would potentially discern different truths about God, and each would be correct.[3] *Core values resonate with daily life.*

BELIEFS

Bedrock beliefs tell the world what you know about God; they clearly state how you see God interacting in the world. That's a new concept for modern, Christendom church leaders. There has been a view in modernity that clarity is tantamount to exclusivity. In a sense that's true, for when you're clear, you don't please everyone. Yet paradoxically, the goal to be inclusive can bring bland narrowness, for in trying to please everyone, you please no one.

---

3. In his book, *Moving Off the Map*, Thomas Bandy talks about using "listening prayer triads" as a way to seek God's vision. His approach is perceived almost as a spiritual discipline, and involves intercessory prayer, meditation, accountability grouping, and discernment.

For example, Christendom churches that have tried to be inclusive have been afraid to make Jesus the focus of Christian worship. If a community believes that Jesus is the incarnation, then it must make him the focus of worship. But if you don't want to offend anyone who might be Buddhist, Muslim, Jewish, or who follow New Age beliefs, you probably won't do much more than teach that Christ is a concept, and thereby you won't talk much about Jesus in the worship moments of your life. Worrying about offending others by clearly stating theological beliefs has caused many Christians to be less than Christian.

Yet the irony is that by being clear, there is room for more diversity than in trying to be inclusive. When a church is clear about beliefs, it leaves the door open for dialogue, and in the dialogue, beliefs can be deepened, even somewhat altered. Communities that clearly state what they believe about God extend an invitation to grow for anyone who is seeking. Bedrock beliefs tell the world who you are and what you and your community stand for; they do not create automatic judgment about another's lifestyle or theological views.

Clearly stated beliefs in God that have the power to transform a community have themselves been grown and fermented in those communities. They are lived out in times of conflict within the community: for example, a bedrock belief in the Incarnation brings compassion into the picture, and offers the potential for peace amid the strife. They are heard in the midst of worship songs, sermons, and liturgies. For example, a bedrock belief in the Incarnation affirms God's presence in life and death and tells us that God offers hope in the midst of suffering. In times of greatest stress, one recalls deepest views about God to remember how he interacts with humanity, to find comfort.

And when there are differences over who God is, and dialogue ensues—be it inside or outside the church walls—God's power can shine through. Sometimes, but not always, differences will mean a parting of the ways between friends or colleagues, as the disparity may be too great. Sometimes it means

that there is an opportunity for those who see things differently to grow and deepen their understanding of God by allowing God to change both sides. But I see the greatest gift to be
when two sides share their bedrock beliefs about God, and
though they may not change their views, they still see God in
each other, and walk side by side in community. This is true
diversity.

Character Development: Motivating Beliefs

It's risky to clearly state your beliefs, because of what might
happen. People might disagree, or even get angry. On the other
hand, you may grow closer. What is the most basic truth you
know about God, that you hold dear, which affects the way you
live your life? *Bedrock beliefs know that God is alive.*

ORIGINS

If I were to speculate about Susan (the lead character introduced at the beginning of this book), I'd imagine that her
bedrock beliefs about God center in his humanity. Her conver-
sion experience was incarnational; every aspect of God on the
cross was a point of connection for Susan in her own life. Jesus
was real to her because he survived suffering and abandon-
ment, and literal death. Jesus lives to show the world God is
alive. Could the same be said now about Susan? *Bedrock beliefs
reveal the first moments in which God became real to you.*

TRIED AND TRUE

God has never rejected me, and he's had plenty of reasons to
do so. In the midst of sin, God has still used me to show others
his compassion; in the midst of fear, God has used me to show
others his power; in the midst of doubt, God has used me to
show others his faith; in the midst of judgment, God has used
me to show others his mercy. As God has shown his generosity
to others, he has changed my heart. I have lain at the foot of the
cross in utter despair and have felt Jesus wash over and through

me. I believe that God is filled with forgiveness because my interactions with him have shown me so. *Bedrock beliefs reveal God's activity throughout the days, months, and years of your life, and into eternity.*

METAMORPHOSIS

And as a result of God's deep compassion, I've changed. *Bedrock beliefs influence the way you live your life.*

COUNT CULTURE

Professor Simei Montiero, who teaches liturgy at a Methodist seminary in Brazil, talks about flying into São Paulo and seeing the smog settled over the city like a hat. She says that the children who grow up there don't get to see the stars at night, therefore metaphors of God that are about the nighttime heavens have no meaning. Culture influences how we see God. How and where you're raised can affect the most basic beliefs about who God is in your life, for if God is real and walks with us, he lives in the midst of culture and context. *Bedrock beliefs reveal God's diversity.*

In Søren Kierkegaard's essay "Fear and Trembling," he discusses Abraham's three-day journey to Mt. Moriah to sacrifice Isaac. Kierkegaard points out that Abraham, the man of vision, is foremost a man of faith, not obedience. If he were only obedient to God's visions, he'd be a tragic figure. No, Abraham has full faith that God will not take Isaac, and full faith that God will take Isaac. Kierkegaard also points out that Abraham's behavior is not only irrational, but offensive, since he never tells Sarah or Isaac what he's about to do. Yet if he were to have told them and were to have been distracted from his mission, then having shared his command from God would have been his sin, since it would have kept him from responding in faith.

VISION

I'd like to begin this section by stating what I think vision isn't, since that may be easier than stating what it is. .

I've been frustrated over the last several years by what I hear from pastors and worship leaders when they talk about their "vision" for a new service. What I often hear is a decision about how the worship service will look, both in terms of style and technology. I've heard similar visions when new church start pastors are talking about their new churches—speaking of both worship and also the building and grounds—before they've even connected with the first worshiper. When I hear such statements, I feel a wall go up inside, because in the past I've observed the communication of this "clear picture" by the visionary lead to the domination of personal will over the body.

The domination is a result of misunderstanding, pride, and power. Part of what I question when I hear detailed claims of God's vision is whether the vision is really from God. I sometimes sense strong personal desire for leadership success and personal glory in the midst of pride from being so clever as to think of such a great idea. Or sometimes I hear pleasure from the visionary that God has chosen to reveal something of great import to him or her. If the vision is self-motivated, it ultimately won't fly, despite strong-willed leaders who can gather a following and implement parts of what they desire through sheer personal drive and organizational ability.

I'm convinced that the visionary is often the last to grasp the true meaning of the vision, since to follow the vision means to focus on faith, and sometimes that obscures other insights. If Abraham's visions weren't about a literal meaning of millions of offspring, but instead were metaphorical, having something to do with God revealing to the world what it means to walk in faith, then Abraham could never have known God's intention, since if he had, his attempts to walk in faith in order to prove God's point would have been contrived.

Perhaps I hear unholy motivations in others because I've dealt with them in myself. Before I really knew God and began leading a life of committed prayer and study, I often had clever ideas that I thought were godly, and often acted on those, even bringing some of them to life. Now that I lead a much more disciplined life, I've come to sense the difference between a brainstorm and divinely inspired pictures of the future.

God speaks in deep metaphor, and even detailed pictures of God's future have layered meaning. The clarity of God's visions isn't as much about the picture that God reveals to the visionary as it is about what happens to the picture, and those who interact with the picture when the visionary and the body live out the vision. In order to live out the vision, it requires one's interaction with the vision, with one another, and with God. The clarity of the vision gradually emerges in the struggle that ensues after revelation.

True vision is difficult and messy. For one to follow God's vision and to engage others in following God's vision requires irrational, sometimes offensive, sometimes extreme behavior, doubt, fear, and much emotion. That's why, when I hear the pride or the pleasure when a visionary speaks of what God seems to be revealing, I mistrust the vision, as the pride reaction doesn't match the reality of the demanding experience.

Following God's vision can be an experience filled with excitement and unmatched intimacy. Still, it will likely include pain for both the visionary and those he or she loves. Faith is the core of vision, and it's a double-edged sword. When humans receive faith, it's not an entirely peaceful experience. The power of the Holy is so very different from human power; it will upend you, and you'll never be the same. Vision is about knowing that God is God and we are not; fulfilling God's vision means allowing God to lead. Therein lies the struggle.

True, godly, corporate visions are not owned; they're shared. The former implies order; the latter implies chaos and change. Participation with the vision can lead to reinterpretation of the vision itself, and then to new and unexpected directions. It's a circular process that can't unfold if a visionary tries to hold the strings. For a vision to truly have power, a visionary has to let it go.

Character Development: Motivating Vision

Vision is paradoxical; though on one hand it's messy, on the other hand, it's careful. In all its many dimensions, true vision is always powerful. Godly vision leads to a new community, transforming complacent spirits into devoted souls. *Godly vision moves people.*

PUZZLE ZONE

In seminars he's led, I've heard Dick Wills tell of his receiving a vision from God for a new community. The vision showed the new community revolving around three things: teaching about Jesus in meaningful ways, relieving suffering, and growing with God in Wesley fellowship groups. Dick notes that people within the new community sometimes receive their own visions of how they are to live their lives for God. To be supported by the church, financially and otherwise, the vision must fulfill one of the three components of the greater vision of the body. Beyond that, a person is free to follow God where he leads, even as he or she remains connected to Christ Church. God interacts with a clear vision on many levels. It's as though the pieces of the puzzle find their own place to fit into the ever-expanding mosaic of God's activity. *Vision organizes and empowers.*

VISION QUEST

God doesn't always insert a vision into someone's head. Often, a person has to seek God's vision. In doing so, it can seem as though God is withholding insight, since the vision doesn't always come right away. When that has happened to me, it has been difficult, but I've learned that my dry and desert times are often God's most fertile moments. God uses my

85

seeking to do something in me that makes me more ready to receive what he has for me. To hear what God has to say, I must pray, wait, and listen. *Vision brings discipline and emotion.*

IMPERFECTIONS

In many ways, I'm a very unlikely person to receive God's visions. I'm not the model of holiness that many would identify as the ideal Christian leader, yet God has seen fit to give me faith and show me pictures of what he sees for the future. I'm not always sure what the pictures mean, but I'm always sure that I need to follow, and I'm always sure that the impact of following will be big. God's visions don't wait for you to be perfect or even ready. They simply take you from where you are and move you forward, changing you and everyone who loves you. Sometimes it's stressful; other times it's almost humorous; always it's miraculous. *Vision has its own power.*

MISSION

I find it difficult to tell the difference between mission and vision. In fact, there's a sense in which all four components of a church's DNA blur together. Unfortunately, in our desire to be obedient servants, most of us get caught up in structure. We want to articulate our DNA correctly, and in the process, we become more concerned with making sure we use the correct definition than with having a mission or vision in the first place. It's helpful to do the exercises that include writing a mission or vision statement, but I personally don't worry much about which is which. In my experience, many mission statements sound like vision statements, and vice versa, depending on whose definition you're using. Still, though a definition for mission or vision may not match mine, the mission or vision statement can be very effective, regardless of which category it fills, since it serves to reveal something about God.

Churches are taught to write a mission statement, a vision statement, values, and a belief statement. They're taught to summarize the mission statement in just a few words so it can be put on a T-shirt for everyone to easily remember. They're taught that a mission statement sounds one way, and a vision statement sounds another way, and that there's a purpose statement, and then a statement of ideology—too many statements.

In exploring mission—like vision—it's a bit easier to see what not to do than what to do. Many churches still try to gain a corporate acceptance of mission by having a committee write the mission statement. The result is a bland statement that has too many words and very little meaning, revealing nothing about what God is seeking to do in people's lives. The reality of mission is that it grows out of the vision, values, and beliefs of a community of faith, and a committee can't come up with that without having been part of the journey of discovery. Further, a committee will try to make mission politically correct, which is the opposite of true mission. Mission is unsafe and demanding, and serves the purpose of tapping into God's transformational power in Jesus Christ.

The paradox is that mission is actually often articulated first, and values and beliefs grow out of a missional calling. Pastors and church leaders sometimes get a very clear sense of mission, that they're to lead a community through transformation, even before they clearly articulate their values or bedrock beliefs, or before they have any picture from God of a direction to follow. Also, true mission in the Christian church isn't really a great mystery, since the mission of every Christian is to lead others to Christ and make disciples.

However, the fact that God works contextually brings nuances. The mission of every Christian and, therefore, every church, is to make disciples. Yet, how is that lived out within a specific cultural context? Vision, values, and beliefs have a bearing on how mission is lived out, which is why they must also influence the mission and mission statement that you will write for your own local church, or ministry, or both. The mission statement not only reveals the truth of God, but keeps people acting on the truth of God. It literally defines the community.

Character Development: Motivating Mission

To effectively lead community change, leaders need a personal mission. They need to know God and love him deeply, be devoted to him, and have deep trust in him. Leading community change can be demanding, if not discouraging. Personal mission can sustain you through it. *Mission captures you.*

INNER STRENGTH

Many church leaders struggle with leading change in their local churches. Leaders are taken over by the sinister drama of people refusing to journey to the promised land; as a result, they sometimes leave their life work in anger and bitterness. Often, the problem is that leaders don't have an unshakable identity in Jesus Christ. Though they may have good ideas and follow the guidelines of change as taught to them by the experts, the deep knowledge of being in Christ is missing. Christian identity drives the need to share Jesus and ultimately determines what you will and won't do. Knowing who you are in Christ doesn't stop the pain if the body refuses to join you, but it keeps you going in the midst of it, or helps you shake the dust off your feet and move on. *Mission is about Jesus.*

RECONCILABLE DIFFERENCES

A leader's personal mission and the church's corporate mission must complement each other. If the leader has a vision for a new community that revolves around changed lives because of knowing Jesus, and the corporate mission statement doesn't speak to the process of transformation, the leader will need to bring about change in the body, which the corporate mission must ultimately reflect. Leaders with a personal vision of transformation can affect that change by working with a core group of leaders who believe in transformation through Jesus. Belief in the new mission comes from the struggle that accompanies the journey of discovery of the corporate DNA, not in actually writing the mission statement. If mission is an outgrowth of vision, values, and beliefs, the community will claim ownership for the mission because of the time it took to articulate the mission and struggle with it. *Mission is transformational.*

CALCULATIONS

When humans follow God into mission, spiritual leadership is at times about tenacity, especially when faith and trust wane, as they sometimes do. The farther you go with God, the greater and weaker your faith becomes as you reach the most basic layers of soulful resistance. Growing in trust often means that our personal resistance to God looms larger than ever, as God prods us deeper into the risky territory of becoming spiritual leaders. Such ambiguity has taught me to scrupulously ignore my insecurities that I've indulged in the past—things that usually have the ability to sabotage godly efforts. I've learned that part of the discipline of turning over my worries to God is actually allowing them to fester, untouched by me. I don't try to fix them; I don't pretend to ignore them. With full awareness of my discomfort, I simply let my worries abide for a time, as they filter through my spirit while I continue about my missional work, for the mission is more important than my insecurities. I've found that God honors my obedience and is faithful with his hope, as he gently lifts up pieces of my struggles here and there, and, with his love, helps me face myself, thereby bringing me into a deeper trust than I had before. *Mission endures.*

STAGE DIRECTIONS

1. Spend some time exploring your values and beliefs with the team you've gathered. Think about answers to the following questions:

- What are your personal values, beliefs, visions, and mission?
- Do your personal values match what you perceive the church's values to be?
- What is missing from the list, in terms of what you *wish* were the values and beliefs of your community?

2. If you were to seek out God's vision among his people in your community by asking them about their lives, what questions would most reveal God's dreams and visions to you? Here are a few ideas to get you started:

- What is the biggest dream of your life?
- If this dream were to come true, what would it fulfill for you?
- What is currently the most fulfilling part of your life?
- What music do you listen to? Who's your favorite group? What is the best concert you've ever attended?
- What is the best movie you've seen in the past six months or year? Why was it meaningful for you? Did it speak at all to God's involvement in the world?

IF YOU'RE STARTING A NEW SERVICE

1. Begin thinking about the profile of the person you believe you're being called to reach in your community. What does this person look like? What are his habits? What movies does she attend? What concerts has he attended? What music does she listen to? Where does he live? What kind of house does she have?
2. How does focusing on the profile of your target market help you think more deeply about values, mission, beliefs, and vision? How does thinking about values, mission, beliefs, and vision help you focus the profile of your constituency?

WORSHIP TEAMS FEEL THE DYNAMISM OF GOD

DIRECTOR'S NOTES

When a person sits in an audience and watches a live perform-ance, he is a part of the performance. Every audience is different, every actor is different, every performance is different. Live the-ater is dynamic. In worship, every designer is different, every worshiper is different, and God interacts with each one as he chooses. Worship, like drama, is dynamic and must be experienced.

VICKY AND SONORA

Going to my daughter's church was a surprising experience. I'm not enamored of Christianity, and I had made up my mind I would-n't like it. But Sonora had been going to a Bible study at her friend's house against my wishes, and I was concerned about her. I thought maybe it was a cult. Her Bible group attends this service on Sunday evenings. Since she wouldn't let me attend her Bible group, the Sunday service was as close as I could get to seeing what might be happening.

I'm still uncomfortable about the Bible group. Perhaps it's just because I can't relate. But I liked several things about the church. The music was just the kind of thing Sonora likes to listen to; it was very good. It was unusual to sit at tables and eat and drink coffee. It was very casual, although it was a little too close for me.

When I entered, I saw larger-than-life crosses in the room, propped up against the four walls. I noticed there were holes all over the front of one of them, and I assumed the rest were like that. I decided the holes indicated nails that had been pounded into the wood on several occasions. My initial reaction was reserved; I'd had enough of crosses growing up. I couldn't imagine what they'd be using them for and I wasn't interested in any more empty ritual.

I was right about the nails. But when we were asked to write our names on a piece of paper and hammer our names to the cross, it didn't seem exactly empty. I didn't go; I just watched. It was stunning to hear all that pounding, and to see people attaching their own lives to what is supposed to be a symbol of eternity. For some, the pounding was intense; for others it was . . . simple. It touched me to see it.

Just before the ritual, there was a young woman who spoke and read some poetry she had written—Susan was her name. She was sweet and pretty—and somewhat decorated with tattoos and piercings, and colorful hair. She spoke so well about her struggle with getting to know Jesus. She was completely honest about how hard it was to let go of her worries and hurts; it was meaningful to hear her express that. I don't remember when I was growing up that anyone ever admitted it was difficult to change even if Jesus was in your life. Our priests would never have said that, nor would they have allowed anyone else to say it publicly.

I really would rather Sonora not have started in on this direction. I don't want her to become just another arrogant, closed-minded Christian. I hope that won't happen.

Though secular, you can learn a lot about the dynamics of worship by watching adolescents and teens reach nirvana at a concert presented by the teen idols of the day. Teens literally abandon themselves to the moment, and from the release of their identity, they gain identity. They become someone new, a meaning that is derived from a connection with those whom they idolize.

> Recently, I watched thousands of teenage girls screaming and swooning, all for the sake of 'N Sync. At that moment, those girls valued 'N Sync more than their own lives. Seeing them reminded me of when I was a teen and a friend of mine brought me to see the Beatles. We were so close to the stage, I could practically touch John Lennon. But I couldn't hear a word the Fab Four sang because everyone, including me, was screaming and swooning.

That, for me, provides two reasons for what happens in worship of the Holy. The first involves letting go of one's identity to gain identity. I believe that's what happens between human and God in worship. The second is the phenomenon of cultural expression, which is how the new identity with God manifests itself. New identity with God and cultural expression are intrinsically connected; each principle reveals and, therefore, influences the meaning of the other dynamic.

In years past, I've heard definitions of worship that include "the response of a called people," "ascribing worth to God," "honoring God," and so forth. It's not that those definitions are wrong; they're just rational, reserved, and removed. In today's world, people want to experience the Holy, so to offer a definition of worship that stays in the head and doesn't open the doorway to a "total experience" is irrelevant.

Abandon is a word that begins to describe what postmoderns desire in a relationship with the Holy. It's an intense word, and filled with expression; it isn't sterile. I'm not suggesting that everyone I know who is designing postmodern worship is using the word *abandon* to describe the dynamic between God and human; however, what I've observed in such worship experiences is representative of just that. It's common in worship that reaches those in their twenties and younger to see very free expressions of love for God. As in a rock concert, young people give themselves over to God in the moment of worship, and gain a new identity. And such behavior isn't restricted to youth, nor is it defined by geography or tradition. I've observed the phenomenon of abandon in many parts of the country, in main-line denominational churches that reach a wide range of ages, as well as in churches I'd call postmodern. The phenomenon is both spiritual and cultural.

But the concept of abandon in worship isn't entirely new. The times I can remember having really worshiped involved the experience of letting go. Whether I entered into worship with walls and God tore them down, or I came in prepared, and God took me to a new dimension, the result was me releasing my own agenda and identity, which brought me to full awareness of myself and full connection to God. Abandon means that God and human are one; one's self is given over to the moment, and in that moment, one's self is simultaneously fulfilled. I still remember those times with clarity.

> One of the most amazing things I've seen in worship is people lying on the ground—not slain in the spirit, just lying on the ground, facedown before God, as an act of humility. The first time I saw someone do that, I did a double take. Then I looked around the room, and I saw that the room was peppered with people lying facedown, praying, absorbing, weeping, bowing before God. I was in awe.

What makes postmodernity different from modernity in worship, however, is the awareness and articulation of the concept of abandon as a valid dynamic of worship, knowing that it will lead to an observable manifestation. Culturally, the idea of abandon simply doesn't fit with the orderly and reserved values of modern worship. If a modern worshiper felt his or her soul go to God, this person would likely not show it so that someone else could actually see it (except in typically charismatic traditions).

In today's world, it's commonplace to see people singing

familiar songs along with their favorite band with their arms raised, eyes closed, bodies swaying, tears streaming down their faces, and to hear laughter, to see clapping, and even to watch people moshing—all in worship. Well, the last item on the list isn't quite as commonplace as the other activities, but it isn't unheard of. What do those things sound like to you?

> Worship is like a string of moments that God can use to bring anyone into a place of consciousness with him. Often, a person will remember an entire hour of worship and praise as a great experience; however, equally as often, God uses a single moment of time to ambush a nonbeliever with the truth of Jesus.

The similarity between worship and cultural events like concerts is striking. And the most fascinating part of this discussion is that not only does releasing one's identity to God lead to a cultural manifestation, but cultural manifestations lead to a new identity with God. I've had friends tell me that they've worshiped at concerts, though some of the concerts have been secular. They may have gone to the concert to worship an idol, but they met the Holy One there, and they weren't confusing their idol with God.

The same phenomenon is true in worship. When a non-Christian watches someone worshiping expressively, the non-Christian will potentially see truth, and want to know more. Also, when a non-Christian is asked to participate in cultural expressions in worship, God will potentially use the activity to reach him or her with the truth. God uses cultural expressions to reveal his love and to bring humans to a place of intimacy with him in which they become brand-new.[1]

---

1. In postmodernity, worship and evangelism are tied together. Worship ties to evangelism by endorsing the reality of God to a nonbeliever; and evangelism ties to worship, since when someone receives Christ, worship is the response. Worship designers often have a hard time connecting worship and evangelism, because modernity has done so well in tearing them apart. *Worship Evangelism: Inviting Unbelievers into the Presence of God* (Grand Rapids: Zondervan, 1999), by Sally Morgenthaler, is a great book to help worship designers understand the connection.

That leads to an interesting dilemma for worship planners, since the term *cultural manifestations* implies secular forms. In today's worship, cultural manifestations include rock music, electronics, and even moshing, among other things. The question for most worship designers is one of boundaries: Just how far do you go with planning for the use of cultural manifestations in worship? And how should you allow them to occur, since cultural manifestations often don't seem to honor a Holy God?

That may be more of a modern than postmodern question, since the shift in thinking from modernity to postmodernity is that in postmodernity, the sacred and the secular are one, whereas in modernity, they are separate. Postmoderns would see the sacred and secular occupying simultaneous time and space—no separation or distinction between the two. And if that is the case, then that which we consider to be both sacred and secular is also neither sacred nor secular. In postmodernity, God doesn't just "work through" that which has been considered either sacred or secular, as most in modernity would have said; God *is* both sacred and secular, at once. And if he is both, then he is also neither.

> A controversial example of the blur between sacred and secular is the film *American Beauty*, which was highly offensive to some; yet, for others, was a vehicle to seeing humanity's need for a savior. The desperation of the film's characters led to what were often perverted behaviors, which horrified many godly viewers. But for others, *American Beauty* was one of the most powerful ways God has ever been revealed in film, or otherwise.

Earlier in this book, I said that postmodern worship was not about "multimedia, multisensory, technology, performance worship, participative worship, or experiential worship," and yet, the twenty-first-century paradox is that worship *is precisely* about those things, because they are the forms of the day and therefore the tools of communication that God will use. Technology and multimedia define today's world and worship. The paradox means that God will use any form to communicate the truth in such a way that one will be unable to separate the form from the truth; the form is as important as the truth. However, God simultaneously devalues the form, and says that to make the truth *about* the form is to miss the entire point, because only God is the truth. God is both sacred and secular, but he is also *neither* sacred nor secular, as his truth is beyond our human understanding of both.

> A live drama is both more and less real than a video on the same topic. A video can profile real people in real-life situations, while in live drama, actors simply portray real people. Yet video is a cool medium and is more distant than live drama, since live drama has physical proximity.

If you've been to the Vietnam Veterans Memorial in Washington, D.C., you may have an idea what I'm talking about. You can look at the wall and be mesmerized by it, or you can enter into the space of it and be taken over by it. If you stand back from it and look at it, you can see that the wall is covered with columns of names. People walk into the space that contains the wall; they touch the indentations on the wall that are the names of loved ones whom they'll never see again on this earth; they trace the names and bring the tracing home with them; or just remember the feeling of the names on the tips of their fingers. People leave flowers or other personal items; they weep, and pray, and comfort each other, and stand alone sometimes too, with nothing but their thoughts and the echoes of the past to haunt them. But even if you know of no one personally who lost his or her life in Vietnam, you can walk into the space that contains the wall and gain an awareness of the feelings and memories of others. You leave a part of yourself there when you visit, and you also take away something that will stay with you forever. It's an eternal experience.

When Jesus was out among the crowds, a bleeding woman came to him to be healed. She touched the hem of his garment. When she did that, he felt some of his power drain out of him, and she was healed. In the meantime, Jairus, a religious leader, was waiting for Jesus to go to his home to heal his daughter. While Jesus was distracted with the bleeding woman, Jairus's daughter died, though later in the story, we read that Jesus raised her from the dead. But Jesus chose first to deal with the outcast, the woman at the fringes, who was the opposite of the churched establishment. Her healing took place on the streets, and led to a public declaration of faith as she told everyone what had happened.

The Vietnam Veterans Memorial is a cultural phenomenon. It is both sacred and secular. It speaks to a time in history that is becoming part of the collective memory of a nation; even younger people who know nothing about the horrors of the Vietnam War can visit the memorial and know something of what occurred in a distant land so long ago. It's a contemporary ritual, revealing the past, present, and future. It is both a work of art to be observed and digested, as well as a vessel that gives people an opportunity to express themselves through action. The people who visit the memorial are a part of the art, as they bring it to life and connect it to current life through all time.

But to get to the depth of it, I believe that the God of Jesus reveals himself in this monument, and that the experience of being there is true worship—not just for me, a believer, but also for those who may not believe in the God of Jesus in the same way I do. That view is possibly difficult for a modern Christian to agree with, since the monument is not claiming to be Christian. A woman named Maya Lin designed the art; I don't know if she's a Christian. Many of the names that appear on the wall represent atheists, agnostics, Muslims, or Buddhists; many who visit fall into those categories too. Yet God is active. And the names of Christians aren't highlighted in any way, but are simply listed side by side with other faith traditions, or with those who had no faith.

Still, when I see the wall and all that it encompasses, I see God's nature. And I think it's possible that others may also see God's nature, even if they can't articulate it, or wouldn't articulate it in the same way I would. The potential exists, as a reality of the art, to bring people to an awareness of the truth of God in Christ, because of the art itself. It brings others and me into a connection with God and one another, and that reality doesn't depend on who sees it or is part of it, or whether or not they can actually articulate it.

Also, the fact that the memorial's focus is outside the church is essential to understanding the art, God, and finally, myself. In today's world, people look for God in everyday life; there is no separation between time and place in order to find God. Knowing God as a result of being in the midst of the Vietnam Veterans Memorial first moves me beyond the art, and takes the focus off the cultural manifestations and into a connection with God. It then brings me back into focus on the cultural manifestations with deeper understanding and appreciation of the beauty and meaning of it. I am deeply connected to God in the midst of it.

In public worship, cultural manifestations operate in the same way as the Vietnam Veterans Memorial. These manifestations show us that God is alive and well in the world, and let us know that God isn't afraid of the world; his power is far greater than anything the world can do or say. Cultural manifestations use all the senses to reach a human heart. They aren't available to us to make a specific point about God that fits a weekly theme; they're available to us to encourage our imaginations about God, and also to show us and the world that God and human form intimate bonds with each other that can't be torn asunder.

God uses whatever is available to say "This is who I am." Both human and God need and seek each other in the context of worship. God needs the intimacy of human relationships as much as humans need God's intimacy, and it's through the use of cultural forms and expressions that intimacy with God happens. When worship designers have known God's intimacy, they seek a cultural manifestation to reveal God's nature to others. But the manifestation is also spontaneous and unplanned as well, for it happens when God empowers it.[2]

> It seems that modernity has forgotten about the eros of God. Rational thought has led moderns to say that godly love is expressed as agape; however, agape doesn't get to the depth of God's passion. Agape relegates the experience of the cross to obedience, whereas God's eros makes the experience of the cross central in God's passionate desire. God's eros is the fullness of every aspect of his love; it's the drive in him that causes him to keep giving himself for us.

The most incredible truth I know about God is that he desires me, and my soul. He wants to dance with me. He created me, and he created you just for that dance. Everything about him speaks to his incredible passion for human beings— his forgiveness, his compassion, his truth, his eternity, his creativity, his mercy, his memory. God is pleased with our cultural expressions of, through, and for him. He became human so that we would know him; our cultural manifestations express that knowledge. God is human and God is God. God is both sacred and secular.

---

2. It might be tempting to see cultural manifestations as contrived in some way, as worship designers often try to manufacture them as a way to evangelize. Cultural manifestations are really God's activity. Whether the manifestation is a work of art, an icon, or another expression of love, God does all the work. We can be assured he will elicit cultural manifestations of his presence in our lives; therefore, it's right to plan for the event to occur.

Worship in the twenty-first century is a powerfully edgy combination of the Holy and the profane. But the depth of the edginess is not from any cultural form or expression in and of itself. It comes from the awareness that we somehow become one with the Holy, that we can and must abandon our identity to him and become new. That's the point. When God knows us and we know him, we experience eternity. That is the dynamism of God that worship leaders need to feel. It will be the foundation of any public worship offering, giving it relevance and authenticity.

Character Development: Cameo

It's fun when directors make a cameo appearance in their own movies. Try to find Alfred Hitchcock (or Stephen King) in every one of his movies. He always appears in a cameo, although trying to find him is a little like trying to find Waldo. It's a statement, though, because the director is saying that he or she is very present. You may not be able to pinpoint exactly where he is, but he's there, feeling what you feel, and influencing what you feel.

Worship leaders appear in their worship too, even if they're only behind the scenes. When worship leaders feel the dynamism of God, they share it, and by sharing it, they influence the expression of it. In a sense, every worshiper has a cameo appearance in public worship. And in a sense, like with the Vietnam Veterans Memorial, the cameo appearances of all worshipers reappear each time the people gather to worship.

BACK TO THE FUTURE

Biblical worship is very expressive, and is reminiscent of manifestations that might occur at a contemporary rock concert. Also, worship offerings today include a return to the use of incense, candles, anointing, laying on of hands, and other biblical ritual and liturgical expressions, which seem to be as culturally relevant now as they were thousands of years ago. We take ancient rituals and make them our own, giving them a new twist in a new context. Part of the value of cultural expression is that it takes us back and brings us forward. It taps into something deeper, connecting worshipers to the identity that has existed in us before time, which is Jesus.

ABRAHAM BUILT AN ALTAR

The most meaningful ancient ritual to include in worship is *worship*. Every time Abraham followed God somewhere new, he built an altar. That which truly ties the ancient to the future is the desire to unabashedly love God in a public setting.

SUPERNATURAL

The discussion of cultural manifestations will probably take most teams to the dimension of the supernatural. God's power is supernatural and, therefore, it's impossible for worship designers to ever fully describe or plan for how God will reveal himself in worship. No one knows what form or expression God will use to reach a human heart.

But if you're going to talk about God's supernatural power, then you have to think also in terms of the dark side of the supernatural. A fascinating component of cultural manifestations in worship is the awareness of the presence of the satanic. As a mainline Christian, talking about the supernatural and God in the same breath is relatively new for me. But add to that any validation of the forces of evil, and the discussion seems radical. However, I've come to know that when God is present, Satan likes trying to invade. Worship that praises Jesus is dangerous. It means that you're always pushing the bounds of good against evil.

Risky though it may be, postmodernity is not afraid to talk about and banish the power of Satan in worship. It has always been true that in worship, people often come face-to-face with their own demons, like anger, hatred, apathy, arrogance, and many others. Worship divines the unholy. Also, there is a sense that worship is the antidote to the powers and principalities of the spirit life. In 2 Chronicles, the worship leaders were the ones to lead the troops into battle, praising God all the way, and repelling the forces of evil that would seek to foil God's Holy victories (20:17-21). In Acts, Paul and Silas sang hymns of praise while in prison and their chains were released, and their jailers were converted by witnessing God's power and miracles. Worship both invites and destroys Satan's power.

IN MY LIFE

The discussion of cultural manifestations must always be contextual and must always consider what is happening already in the lives of the people in the community in which the worship experiences are taking place. Who lives there? What are the styles of the people? What are the burning issues of a person's life? What are the burning issues in the life of a large and small community of people? What is happening in the hearts and minds of people that is defining their existence? Who is planning the worship? Who is leading the worship? What are the gifts and graces of the worship leaders? What is the ethnic background of the people in the community? What minority cultural influences have begun to be noticed in the midst of the dominant cultural experiences of the community? What kind of blur between American culture and immigrant culture is taking place? How is music, style, the arts, culture, lifestyle, leadership, personnel and all that "is" working together to reveal God? All are questions addressing God's activity in a cultural context.

STAGE DIRECTIONS

How do cultural manifestations build the team of worship designers? Part of the answer to this question is "awareness." Worship designers simply need to be thinking about cultural manifestations—what they mean and how they reveal God. But worship designers need also to have experienced God in worship, in their own hearts. Cultural manifestations represent transformation. So each worship designer needs to be able to answer the following questions: How has God transformed my own life in worship? What has been the most significant worship experience of my life, and why was it so powerful? What were all the components of that experience that brought me face-to-face with God?

The danger in this exercise is that worship designers will begin to assume that the manifestations and forms of worship that affected them are *the same ones* that will be important for everyone. Worship design is a tightrope walk. It's essential that worship designers feel the dynamism of God, and it's important that they detach from their own connection with God's power when designing worship. Worship design is never about "me." Though we may want to repeat the experiences that helped us meet God face-to-face, or be tempted to see the rest of the world from our own vantage point, self-reflection is only a stepping-stone to the greater awareness of God's activity in the greater community.

Self-reflection in worship is important. It will help the worship designer see more about God; it will bond worship designers to one another and to the greater community as they share the ways in which God has been working in their lives; and the process of self-reflection will lead to setting one's personal needs aside for the greater good of the community. As we move into the discussion of indigenous worship later in this book, it will become essential that the team members begin to reach the depth of connection between self, one another, and God with regard to their own salvation history through worship.

What I'm suggesting is that worship designers learn to tell their own story. In churches in which there are mighty worship wars, there is often arrogance over the right way to worship. The arrogance is motivated by defensiveness, competitiveness over differing needs, or control. Regardless of the cause, the result is the same. However, if people actually listen to God's power through worship, learn to tell what they heard, and also listen to what others heard from God in the context of worship, God can reveal his own diversity, and then pride and judgment are free to take a backseat.

Begin to practice your story by answering the following questions for yourself, and then share them with the team:

- When was the first time you remember meeting God face-to-face in worship? Or describe the most powerful worship experience you've ever had.
- What happened that made God real to you?
- What was happening in your life prior to this experience?
- What were some of the components of worship that you think facilitated the process of worship for you?
- What were some of the surprises? That is, would you have expected "thus and so" to have actually been the thing that made the difference in your worship experience?
- What was God doing that day?
- What are the principles of God's dynamism that you can learn from your own and others' experiences?

IF YOU'RE STARTING A NEW SERVICE

It's not too soon for your team to begin worshiping together. There are several ways to do this as a small community. The principal way would be to think about your target constituency and then start gathering music and other art forms that you think would have meaning to this group of people, and develop worship accordingly.

- One option would be to begin buying CDs of artists who appeal to your target group. Write out words to songs on a page and sing with the songs on the CD.
- In addition to buying CDs, you may want to visit a local Christian bookstore and buy some music books, or peruse a Web site that has music and other resources.
- Perhaps you could write some songs, liturgies, or dramas aimed at your target audience.
- Make a talisman or symbol that you think represents the community you're trying to reach, and discuss the meaning of it.

Be creative. No form or specific expression is right or wrong, but all expressions have differing degrees of meaning and effectiveness.

WORSHIP TEAMS WATCH
CULTURAL TRENDS

DIRECTOR'S NOTES

When you watch Shakespeare's works being performed, you see period costumes, hear certain language that isn't common today, hear accents, and see scenery that looks different from the way current housing and commercial property appear. Good actors try to understand and replicate the culture in which the drama is occurring. If they don't, the drama won't feel authentic. Worship designers are faced with the same challenge, since it's in the midst of culture that people meet God.

DANIEL

Sonora told me that she didn't tell her mom everything they do at her Bible study, because her mom would freak. I can see why. It was—otherworldly. And if you only heard about it and didn't experience it for yourself, you'd think they were wasted.

Sonora knew I was coming home on break, so she e-mailed me to come with her. We're really good friends, and I wanted to see what was up. She seemed so different. She used to be a little cold. Once you got to know her she wasn't that way, but it was hard to get to know her.

I still haven't figured out why she started going to that Bible study, except one of her really good friends went there, and she just kept bugging Sonora about going. I think Sonora originally thought it would be another way to be better than others. But now she has this, like, gentleness. She doesn't seem as stuck-up. She seems more open, more natural.

I must admit, though, it was pretty freaky. At one point this Russ guy got a "word of knowledge"—that's what he called it—about Steve, one of the older guys in the group, whose knee was still kind of messed up after surgery three months ago. Russ said that during the prayer God spoke to him and told him he wanted to heal Steve, and that right after that, his—Russ's—hands were feeling hot. Then Steve got in the center of the room, and everyone put their hands on him, and Russ put his hands on Steve's knee and prayed.

Now I swear to God, I would not have believed it if someone just told me about it. But Steve was limping when he came in to the meeting, and he got up from that prayer and he was moving a whole lot better. Sonora says that this kind of thing has happened before. I really wondered if they planned it, but she swears she didn't know it was going to happen before it happened. She says that's how the Holy Spirit works. The Holy Spirit? What is that?

My mom said that Sonora's group is Pentecostal. My mom was raised Lutheran, a little-known fact to her Wiccan friends. Sonora turns up her nose at Wicca, but it isn't evil. The Blair Witch Project was not representative of Wicca. It is supernatural, though. I think it's interesting that both Sonora and my mom worship something supernatural. Are their gods really that far apart? Sonora says they are—something about the word incarnation. *To her it's actually about life and death.*

When I think back on that whole evening, I wonder, Did it really happen? Sonora gave me a Bible to take back to school with me. She just got baptized. I think that sounds cool.

Not long ago, I was driving in downtown Minneapolis during rush-hour traffic. I happened to look up and saw one of those billboards with moveable panels. One set of panels said "Now and Zen," and had a picture of a high-tech American city with a picture of an ancient Chinese edifice superimposed on it. Then the panels changed, and the next sign was for a major airline advertising travel to the Orient.[1]

---

1. I wonder if I could see a sign like this today. Since September 11, 2001, much has changed. A billboard featuring tall buildings and an airplane could be greatly misconstrued. What I realize as I consider those thoughts is that in the twenty-first century, our world changes very quickly.

I love that sign, because it is so very clearly a product of the emerging postmodern culture. It is *not* a Christendom sign. A Christendom sign would very likely not be using spirituality to catch someone's attention. And if a Christendom organization did, the focus wouldn't be Zen Buddhism. In a Christendom culture in which everyone is considered to be Christian, it would be a huge offense to do so.

The sign is a true sign. I'm not an expert on sociological trends, but I've observed that we no longer hear about Christianity in schools, textbooks, movies, politics, on television, or in other aspects of everyday life in the way we used to during modernity. I've noticed that in some parts of the country, Christianity is still a fairly strong influence, while in many parts of the country it isn't. And in the areas where it still is influential, that's slowly changing. Further, children aren't growing up in the church in the same numbers that they were in modernity, except, again, in certain parts of the country. Postmodern people generally are more interested in the spirituality they can get by going directly to the source, like China, where they can experience the mystique of Zen.

> For some who may have seen that sign, there may have been anger; for others, apathy. I've seen both reactions to the type of information that billboard gives us, and both are different aspects of the denial churched people feel at the dramatic impact of cultural changes on everyday life and on changing the way people feel about Christianity today.

The billboard was so intriguing visually because it had a beautiful, modern-looking city with an ancient city in the midst of it. That's the contrast and concurrence of life today. It is both *ancient and future*, and the ancient and future are but a short airspace apart. We want depth, and we can get it by going to the place with the cool-looking ancient house. Going there is easy to do in today's world, because we're so global and the technology is so accessible that it makes the world a much smaller place. The cities of the future and of the ancient past are neighbors. The billboard didn't advertise classes in Buddhism or anything like that; it was just telling you how to get there and what it would be like when you did. Getting there will probably be enough for most folks, but who knows? Maybe some might wind up staying, just because they can.

What's happening culturally in America today and in the world and what does any of it have to do with worship design?

A term that will help worship designers decipher cultural trends is "pre-Christian." Postmodernity is pre-Christian. That means that the era that follows modernity, or postmodernity, has more in common with life two thousand years ago, when Jesus was first born, died, and rose again, than it does with the entire era that has preceded it for the last five hundred years. It also means that new Christians today are more like the early Christians of the Bible than they are like Christians of twenty or two hundred years ago. It means that there are cultural influences that have changed the views of the world toward life and church, and that worship designers need to be aware of these important attitude shifts, as they affect not only cultural manifestations, but the content of worship itself.

I have heard the term "post-Christian" used to describe post-modernity, but I don't find that terminology as descriptive as "pre-Christian." Post-Christian seems to imply that the era we are in is after Christianity, which isn't entirely true. One could also take that to mean that we've had Christianity and now it's over, which doesn't describe the phenomenon of Christianity in postmodernity. In this pre-Christian culture, it isn't as though people know Jesus and are rejecting him. In the parts of the country where you see large nonchurched populations, people don't know Jesus, period. They have no context to discuss him, and no experience with him either spiritually or theologically to make him real in any way. The term "pre-Christian" describes that phenomenon well. It makes me think in terms of something that's emerging, as opposed to something that was heard and rejected and is now dead.

I recently did a search on the Web for "cult," and got a list as long as my arm. What intrigued me about it was that very few, if any, of the cults were satanic or particularly dark sounding in any way. They were mostly either intellectual and experiential, or occasionally odd and silly sounding. Today's pagans are neither third world—barbarians nor unsophisticated bumpkins; they're not kooks or evil or demonic; they're not angry—not any more than some people who call themselves Christian. And they're not really experimenting. Polytheism is a way of life.

In today's world, Christ is emerging as though he had just walked this earth, having been born of Mary, having lived his thirty-three or so years, and having just been crucified, buried, resurrected, and taken into heaven. It's an amazing phenomenon, because he's emerging into a culture that is almost a mirror for the time in which he actually did walk this earth. The pre-Christian culture of two thousand years ago was pagan, and polytheistic. There were many gods. That is also true today. The pagan/polytheistic environment in which the local church is called to exist is growing in both size and influence.

The pagan influence is both exciting and frightening. It's exciting, because there is so much potential for bringing new life to people as we introduce them to Jesus for the first time. Christianity flourished in the pagan world of the book of Acts. It's frightening because the images that paganism conjures up are largely negative. Also, the truth of the world around us is so significantly different from what any of us "churched folk" can imagine that it seems as though we're in a foreign land.

It's important to think through what paganism looks and feels like, because it is influencing the ways in which people are coming to Christ today. Most of us probably associate very expressive if not orgiastic and cultish behavior with paganism. Not all pagans are involved in cults, but cults are an example of pagan culture. Many cults worship with ritual, chant, and other forms and manifestations that serve to bring the participants into an altered state of consciousness, so that there can be a strong experience of something mystical. That sounds a lot like Christian worship today as well.

> I had a fascinating experience while out with some friends. We ran into a young man who was a former member of a youth group led by someone in my group of friends. This young man had never been mainstream, seemingly rejecting Christianity. Now he lives in what he calls a "ministry house." He took us there to meet the other young adult residents. They are devoted to Christ; they either work or go to school and tithe any money they have; they know the Bible better than most seminary students; they pray daily and break bread together; they pray for their city and worship weekly with a larger community—the twenty-first-century house church.

If you read the book of Acts, you can learn a lot about the pagan culture of the first century of Christianity, and how Christianity developed in the midst of it. Futurists have told us to expect the house church to reemerge as we move further into the twenty-first century. Think of what the house church offers to a new Christian: close relationships, opportunities to talk deeply about what it means to be a Christian, mentoring from someone more advanced, the opportunity for breaking bread together, the freedom to experience God with cultural manifestations that are "in the moment," without judgment from someone who doesn't relate, the freedom to be apart from the world. The house church is an aspect of cultish Christianity. It is a lifestyle of worship.

Also, the house church provides Christians with the hope that their community won't become dead and lifeless—like so many churches have become in modernity—as a result of being entrenched in bureaucracy and hypocrisy. I'm not suggesting that all churches in the twenty-first century will be house churches; however, like the house church, postmodern local churches are thriving and will continue to thrive because they reject the hierarchy and machinery of the Christendom model church that has characterized modernity. The concerns of the postmodern church are and will continue to be nothing like the concerns of the Christendom church.

> The house church is not to be confused with small-group ministries. Small-group ministries in many (though not all) churches are part of a mechanical structure that identifies them with modernity. Modernity has built small groups on an organizational model of multiplication; groups split off to get more people involved, making the mechanics often seem more important than the hopes and dreams of the people. "Small groups" seem to imply that there's a large group somewhere, and in postmodernity, that may not be the case, as worship is getting smaller as well as larger. The house church won't likely exist to multiply and divide as a part of a system of growing a local church.

When I think of a Christendom church, I think of "club." There are people who are in, and people who are out, and the ones who are in aren't interested in the ones who are out. You can fit into a Christendom church when you look like others in the church and when you know what do to when you get there. If you are too far outside the status quo, the club members may see you as charity, and try to change you to look and be like them. Or they may reject you and keep their distance.

Christendom churches are more concerned with voting on the color of the carpeting (or on whether or not to start a new worship service) than with helping God soften a human heart. Voting is club behavior; it equals control. Christendom churches operate on control and predictability. It's more important to have control than to change and be changed. Transformation is not a value of Christendom.

House church participants disdain the Christendom church. They find Christendom Christians to be hypocritical and shallow. They disdain the hierarchy and machinery of the Christendom church, finding power inappropriately in the hands of a few who neither know nor care about Jesus. Some think that the rebellion against the status quo is a cultural pendulum, much like the 1960s, when kids rebelled against the establishment. They expect the pendulum to swing back again. That thinking is a mistake.

In the Christian Club, members consider themselves to be stakeholders, and therefore responsible for all activities. Decisions are made by the leadership in Christendom churches to please and appease the stakeholders, lest they withhold money and the budget of the church begin to falter. The machinery of the Christendom church is more important than the mission of the church. The Christendom church revolves around the maintenance of the machinery, which gives the stakeholders their identity.

In Christendom, there is a right way and a wrong way to worship; the wrong way is any way that is different from the way worship has been led for however many years the stakeholders have been present. Christendom churches value inclusiveness to the point that it's forbidden to say or do anything that will upset anyone, thereby creating the most boring, bland, and exclusive places on the planet. By the way, inclusiveness doesn't include different styles of worship in Christendom churches.

Christendom churches don't believe that the culture has changed as vastly as it has. They believe that most Americans have come from a Christian background. They do not appreciate the powerful influence of diverse spiritualities on our current culture. Such influences have meant that increasing numbers of people are not being raised in the church, and that even if someone claims to be Christian, he or she may never have had an experience of Jesus. Yet Christendom people believe the world hasn't changed because their world hasn't changed. As a result, they believe that everyone who's new in their church knows Jesus and knows the rules, and they're right, because those are the only people who come there. That's why their churches are dying.

Christendom churches can be established, mainline, denominational churches; they can be established nondenominational churches; they can be established denominational churches of any kind; or, they can be brand-new start-up churches of any denomination or nondenominational tradition. Christendom churches never get out of the cycle of focusing on the machinery of the church and all that goes with it, and start-up churches are very susceptible to that phenomenon.

How can a Christendom church ever reach a non-Christian who has no real knowledge or experience of Jesus, who has a great repertoire of spiritual resources, who may have dabbled in Wicca or Buddhism, who may have studs and tattoos, who may be fifty or fifteen, who wants to find something deep and meaningful in life with an experience that will be more real than the recent tongue piercing he or she got? The Christendom model church of modernity and the needs of the postmodern person are at the opposite ends of the earth.

What characterizes the postmodern church is unabashed clarity about Jesus—who he is and why he is important in one's life. You will be able to see Jesus in me and in the people around you, because he's alive and vital, and has changed me to my core. There is no question that he died and rose again for me, my craziness, my neurosis, my sin, and that he seeks me with all his amazing power and love. He seeks us all in this way.[2] It's

---

2. In his book, *Ancient-Future Faith: Rethinking Evangelicalism for a Postmodern World* (Grand Rapids: Baker Books, 1999), Robert Webber calls this "classic Christianity." He shows the progression of Christian teaching throughout shifts in culture and clearly connects twenty-first-century theology with first-century theology. If you've been thinking postmodernity is a fad, Webber will change your mind. In the first few centuries of Christianity, the power of God was in *Christus Victor*: good triumphs over evil. Postmodern Christians understand that as well as first-century Christians did, though some moderns see it as dualism. But the first apostles were able to convert and baptize pagan communities to become Christian—not by the use of systematic theology, rather by the drama of the Resurrection, the fullness of which can only be expressed in terms of the contrast of life and light over death and darkness, or good against evil.

this clarity that drives the postmodern church, the structure, the values, the focus, the mission, the ministry, the worship, and the people. In postmodernity, I am more concerned with helping you find out why experiencing Jesus will make a difference in your life than I am about getting my own needs met. I have Jesus; he meets my needs. I don't need to control the environment to be satisfied.

Postmodern churches will do whatever it takes to share the gospel message in every ministry, including worship. Style doesn't matter except in that it serves to bring a newcomer deeper into a relationship with Jesus. This is the reason it's so important for worship designers to watch cultural trends, because they speak about what reaches people, and what helps them express their hopes and dreams. All of culture is God's vehicle.

But make no mistake—watching cultural trends isn't about finding the exact communication tool to use in spreading the gospel; that would be a mechanical approach. Watching cultural trends as a way to find a communication tool is superficial, even though the process of watching may lead to exactly that.

The point and true power of watching cultural trends is learning to listen, "being still and knowing that I am God." Watching cultural trends is like being part of a continuously unfolding plot, which helps worship designers and leaders become familiar with God's world so as not to be overtaken by it. Style watching is a source of communion for worship designers; it's a way to see God at work in his own world.

The question worship designers need to continue asking is, "What is God doing in the midst of this expression or that?" Culture changes people and people change culture, and God is in the midst of all of it.[3]

---

3. In *Ancient-Future Faith,* Webber quotes Paul Lakeland, author of *Postmodernity: Christian Identity in a Fragmented Age,* who wrote: "Eschatologies that imagine that the spiritual can have a reality aside from the material are simply naïve" (p. 27). How do you interpret what Lakeland wrote? What might your interpretation mean for the way in which you design worship?

Character Development: Mime

Marcel Marceau, the famous French mime, has always fascinated me. His awareness of people was astutely evident in his theater dance (miming). He expressed so much detail without words; his ability to notice and articulate nuance was unsurpassed. He is now nearing eighty (as I write this book), and still performing. I hear that he has not mentored anyone into his craft. Yet the nature of his craft is in itself the mentoring tool, for those who would be gifted at mime could watch videos of him telling his stories and learn how to do what he has done. I think Michael Jackson would make a great mime.

Worship leaders are mimes. We watch and share culture in ways that are nonverbal. The ability to stand back and see God in the midst of culture is an art in itself. It takes discipline and keen observation, and the ability to discern truth in the midst of what has been seen. It also takes faith to know that God has something he desires to share, which he reveals contextually in everyday life experiences.

WORSHIP DANCE

Postmodernity is affecting minority cultural changes, gender issues, music and the arts, subcultures and groups, lifestyle, entertainment—and all those things are affecting postmodernity. It is very difficult to characterize postmodernity by any one style or specific cultural influence or issue.

Understanding postmodernity doesn't mean having a corner on the way to communicate with the culture, since there is more than one way. The greater value is to recognize that the culture is changing, and that change is the constant. Postmodern worship will embrace change; change is the dance of worship.

UNMARKED BILLS

Christendom is dead. Christendom churches will not flourish in the twenty-first century. One of the characteristics of Christendom is denominationalism. Trying to develop worship that is denominationally focused in order to honor denominational values will not have meaning in postmodernity. However, there may be tradition within the denomination that can have great meaning to a postmodern person, which will be worth exploring. Tradition isn't dead, as long as there is a contextual or cultural understanding and meaning that accompanies its use in worship. Meaningful, substantive worship is nondenominational.

WORSHIP ART

The early church produced memorable art, and most of it told the story of Jesus' life. We see much of that in stained glass, which can be very attractive to postmoderns since it tells a story to a generation of people who prefer visuals over print. In the early church, people didn't read because they didn't know how. In today's world, we "read" differently from the way we used to. The material we "read" is shorter (sound bites), electronic (on the Internet), aural (we listen to news), and obtained quickly (dipping in and out of magazines and skimming stories).

With art, you get the story and you get much more; you get the heart—fast. Art is experiential; it involves all the senses with immediacy. It's an intuitive expression of a person's thoughts and emotions, which takes us to the "fringes" of our own existence, where we often meet God. Paintings, sculpture, music, movies, videos, poetry, and other forms of art can speak volumes that words alone or concrete and linear thoughts cannot express. For a nation of nonreaders, that's important. Art in worship is becoming a very important tool again.

> My older son has a tattoo and got his tongue pierced. He calls that body art. The tattoo identifies a band he really likes; it's very colorful and also symbolic. The tongue stud is another story. I asked him why he did it, and he replied, "Why not?" There you go. It's jewelry. I've thought about getting a tattoo. If I ever get the courage to get one, it will be a cross with music notes on it.

But does the art need to be religious to be included in worship? What if the art is dark and depressing? Poetry can be like that. What if the poem uses "earthy" language? Some postmoderns tend to talk a little like sailors, even the ones who love Jesus and live a disciplined Christian life. Language is cultural. Would any of this type of expression offend your sensibilities, especially in worship?

If you begin opening your worship to artistic expression, you will be faced with many questions of boundaries, since art is in the eyes and ears of the beholder. What if art includes a nude, similar to that found in the Sistine Chapel? Or contemporary photography like one sees in art museums? Is that pornography? How do you know? How will you develop the genetic code in your congregation to deal with such issues if you are offering worship that attracts postmoderns, for whom art is a key form of communication? Will what you develop be your DNA, or will it be censorship?

ART TECH

Art is a craft, and requires skill and expertise. Art has always required the use of the tools available to create the art, which leads to honing and technique, knowledge and creativity, as well as inspiration. You have to study, practice, and learn new forms.

> The Vietnam Veterans Memorial, which I discussed in the previous chapter, is both a technological and artistic masterpiece. The artist, Maya Lin, is also an architect.

Technology is very influential, especially in the arts. Today's art is often computer generated. If you're a choreographer or a composer, computers not only make your job easier, they give you more options for creativity. Imagine doing the choreography for the Olympics or the Super Bowl halftime show by scratching it out on a piece of paper, compared to doing it on a computer. Further, the computer is another medium of expression in and of itself, different from a canvas, and it actually influences the formation of art in a different way than a canvas would.

Recently I saw a documentary on the origins of human life, in which the central question was, "What allowed some of the first human communities to survive, while others didn't?" The answer: the use of tools. By studying the caves people lived in, scientists learned that thriving communities used tools as technology for their advancement. They applied them to daily living, as well as to making jewelry and art. The art was shared among people and among different tribes, and served to advance the culture. Scientists found that pictures on the caves depicting people herding animals and acting in their daily lives were primitive signs that humans understood their role in the world. The art showed deep thinking and the ability to see outside themselves, as though they were watching themselves in a film.

But technology is tricky, because it's so accessible. Many churches today use technology as the focus, instead of as a way to develop both art and the artist. It's a subtle but very important distinction, and should be an important caveat for worship designers as they consider using technology in worship.

STAGE DIRECTIONS

1. Consider and discuss some of the following questions:

   - What do you see as the boundaries of art?
   - What makes art "art"?

- Who are your favorite artists in some of the different categories of art?

2. Select a psalm and read it together. Now rewrite the psalm and share your poetry with one another.
3. Think about someone who is somewhat connected with your church, but really at the fringes—perhaps a member's child, a friend, or acquaintance. If this person were to participate in the second part of this exercise with you, what would his or her poem be like and why? Would you consider asking him or her to offer such creativity in worship?

IF YOU'RE STARTING A NEW SERVICE

Do you have one or more teams gathered at this time? If you have more than one, are you all meeting together to worship and to share what you've learned about your church's DNA? How do you see your team structure unfolding?

WORSHIP TEAMS PLAN AND LEAD INDIGENOUS EXPERIENCES OF THE HOLY

DIRECTOR'S NOTES

A script is thoughts on a page that have no meaning until they're read or acted out. The writer of the script may have had something in mind, but once the ink is dry, the author has no more control. The rest of the drama team, who give their own unique spin to what they produce, now owns it. Therefore, every production of every script is different. Worship is just like that. We who worship do so within the cultural context of our own lives and communities, and within the specific circumstances of our individual and corporate journeys, making each worship experience different from the next. Worship designers have no ultimate control over the experience.

CHYNNA

It was a holy moment to be with Susan as she heard about Jesus for the first time. It was like God just opened the door. No one was around us; it was totally quiet. It was like I could hear her thinking. Just looking at her face was incredible. She was in awe. I could see her connecting herself to Jesus and receiving his arrows. And God let me be a part of that. It was in the moment. I could never have planned for it to happen the way that it did. God rules.

She and I are so different, even though I'm only about five or six years older than she is. I knew she'd really like Sunday night, even though it's just not for me. Susan has never gone to church, and I was a church achiever. She likes Sunday night because it's not huge like Sunday morning. I don't like Sunday night because I can't hide as well. She likes the hands-on stuff they do at night, the ritual stuff. I don't mind it once in a while, but my cousins were all Catholic growing up and I wasn't, which was always a bone of contention between us. I wound up disliking their worship, and even now, anything that reminds me of it rubs me the wrong way. And I get so caught up in the music we sing in the morning, song after song, it just takes me away. That's how I worship. Susan really dislikes our music; she thinks it's sappy. And she hates the huge crowd. Her worship isn't really that small, but it's much smaller than mine.

Actually, my husband likes Sunday night too. He feels the same about it as Susan does. We usually worship at different times, he and I. Sunday night worship seems to attract a lot more of the recovery people; there are some people from the prison ministry there too. I think most of the Sunday night worshipers would feel really out of place on Sunday mornings. There are only a few NA friends who come to my service. It's just a different experience.

The banners that Susan and I looked at together are right outside the worship space. We all use the same space, but the room gets completely transformed between morning and evening. Yet the purpose is the same, and it's like those banners symbolize that. I used to walk by those banners and never really notice them. They're really cool, but still, they never had the meaning to me they have now. Who'd have thought that just looking at the story of Jesus' life as it came out of someone's interpretation could change someone else's life?

There is no "correct" way to worship. In postmodernity, if worship centers on Jesus, all else is negotiable, because meaningful worship is indigenous.

How does one define indigenous worship? Simply stated, indigenous worship grows out of a church's DNA. It exists to simultaneously reach up, in, and out. It draws upon the gifts and callings of God's people to develop worship in the context of the local church.

I see more layers in the definition than that, however. I find truly indigenous worship to be organic, because as the community changes, indigenous worship reflects those changes. God's

> "Indigenous worship" is fast replacing the term "contemporary worship." The latter has caused battles in the local church, because no one knows what it means; the definition is subjective. Also, the implied value is superiority over anything that's traditional, making established musicians feel like second-class citizens. "Indigenous" encourages variations in worship among local churches, and it doesn't force a choice between contemporary and traditional.

interaction has the potential to change the worship offering as does the influx of new leadership, the participation of the congregation in worship, and the desire to reach those not yet in worship.

Recognizing change as a layer of meaning for indigenous worship opens up a potential can of worms for worship planners. Indigenous worship is indigenous, in part, because it allows for public worship offerings to be influenced by the gifts and callings of those inside the church. The worry is that in allowing worship to be changed by the presence and leadership of "internal" artists, it may become ingrown, watered down, or poor quality, and thereby lose its missional focus.

I do think there's a danger. It takes talented leadership to challenge artists to grow their gifts in new ways. And it takes mature leadership to develop a community of worship leaders and planners who aren't self-centered, and who don't try to manipulate worship offerings to suit their own needs. Worship is a discipleship ministry, and disciples focus on mission. Conversely, artists tend to be sensitive and possessive, and it's sometimes difficult to get them to focus on mission before their need for affirmation and desire to control creative offerings to reflect their personal tastes. Consequently, if you have decided that you're trying to reach a certain segment of the population, and you've identified a certain style of music to use in worhip that represents that population, you may determine you need to find the right talent to pull it off instead of risking working with artists in your midst who may not like your choices.

It's a fine line that artists walk between detaching enough and detaching too much from their work. If artists go too far, then they've probably lost their passion, and art is art because of the passion that's expressed in it. However, it's also true that artists need to be able to let go of what they do, partly because art is subjective, and partly because anything one does as a person of faith in Jesus ultimately belongs to God.

Worship leaders need to be adaptable and use their gifts for the sake of mission, which sometimes means learning new skills and styles. If they're not able, they probably aren't suited to the ministry. But if they are able, it's still a messy process, since learning new styles often creates a blur of styles rather than the replication of a specific style. If you're defining "indigenous" as "targeted," and expecting to make your worship sound and look just like the well-known Gen-X ministry down the road, it won't happen the way you think if you work with the gifts of those God has sent and will be sending your way.

I struggle with targeted, "niche" worship. I find it a great myth that you actually know whom you'll attract because of the careful thought you've put into planning your worship experience. Someone is reading this and saying, "That's not true. You can get boomers with praise, and Gen-X with rock, and. . . ." I've seen some evidence of that, but in truth, Gen-X music is often "praise rock." We make too many assumptions about which generation likes what kind of music. For example, many boomers *also* like "praise rock," which has a sharper edge than the praise music by which many boomers are identified. Musical tastes aren't as segmented as we try to make them.

However, some churches have done very well by copying the indigenous ministries of famous megachurches. Churches that have successfully used well-known ministries as their models for reaching the nonchurched non-Christian through worship have shown the world that there are things that identify boomers

Easum, Bandy & Associates consultant and cyber-friend Paul Nixon, of Gulf Breeze United Methodist Church near Pensacola, Florida, says that to reach twenty-five- to thirty-five-year-olds, you need to put them in charge. He says that their agenda must be taken seriously if they are to be engaged by a worship ministry; it must be not only *for* them but also *by* them at every level.

and Gen-Xers that translate from location to location around the country, making it very appealing to do formulaic worship. (I'm not saying that the megachurches are formulaic, necessarily, but that observers can and will find in megachurch ministries a formula that will carry to another location.)

Churches that set out to copy a famous megachurch's worship may even be utilizing the megachurch's chosen approach as an outgrowth of their own genetic code, finding that the type of ministry for which the megachurch is known would also suit their local community and speak to their own beliefs, values, and vision for worship. The bonus of using a known method is that there's a track record proving it will work.

Perhaps utilizing another church's approach is not all bad. On the other hand, there's a subtle connection to Christendom values when a new worship ministry tries to copy a successful, established worship ministry. Christendom has dictated style and form in worship. Though some well-known worship ministries are nontraditional, to copy them is to assume that there is one style or form that is correct or better.

Have you ever seen the demographic profiles that make recommendations for the kind of music and worship that will attract the various demographic groups? In almost every case, the recommendation is for traditional worship. A commenter on a mailing list server quipped recently, "If the demographic recommendations were correct, our churches would be full."

Also, it's tempting for worship planners to make assumptions about constituencies to try simplifying the work of worship design. Part of the reason megachurches have been successful is that they *didn't* go for the easy approach. They were trailblazers, and developed thriving ministries that grew out of a powerful struggle with God. Their ministries were indigenous because they began with creativity and innovation, and they used the gifts and talents of the community to develop a ministry that would push the bounds of experience beyond what had been done before.

What is most meaningful for me as an observer of megachurches is not the specific worship style or big numbers and great resources, but the willingness of key leadership to take risks. That's postmodern. Just attempting to develop indigenous worship and other indigenous ministries is risky, and a major shift from modernity. (Modernity values sameness, and risk taking leads to differences.)

On the other hand, some established megachurches don't have the edge they once did in worship, and that makes me wonder if their worship is still indigenous. Indigenous worship will change as the community changes. It can't help doing so. However, megachurch worship from some very well-known megachurches is seemingly unchanging.

In that sense, some megachurch worship seems more modern than postmodern, as there is a predictability that comes with it. I have a hunch that even megachurches focus on their own format, because many may believe it's the format that has worked so well to fulfill the mission. And as a result of focusing on format, creativity may have become established and formatted too. My question would be, Is it really the format that has made the difference in reaching out, or is it something deeper?[1]

---

1. I often lead workshops on designing contemporary worship or drama ministry. In the past, I've coached leaders to think thematically with their art. This has changed. Modernity made it voguish to have a weekly drama, testimony, special reading, or video clip, which is a formatted approach. I have nothing against using such contemporary forms. I only object to the view that it must be done every

An unbalanced focus on format can limit God's ability to draw upon the deeper gifts and callings of those who are involved in the design team, by eliminating the opportunity to form deep relationships through creativity. When creativity becomes established, it blocks the deeper journey, which is really the source of creativity. When a team struggles to understand the deeper view, God unearths creativity, and creativity unearths God, like a volcanic eruption. Creative relationships are God's source of fertility for interacting with a community of faith in worship.

Also, the focus on format can serve to limit God's ability to reach others who are not yet a part of the worship arts ministry,

There's a difference between form and format. Form enhances art, such as poetic forms, or the verse/chorus form of some songs. In worship, certain liturgical forms, like responsive readings, can be dramatic and give deeper meaning to what would otherwise be a "conversation." Also, the language and timing of the responsive dialogue can give a variety of feelings to a simple form. Format, on the other hand, tends to increase the predictability of the form. Using a responsive reading at the beginning of each worship service is a format. The challenge of formatting is to keep the form interesting and new, week after week. Formatting can be meaningful, as it underscores repetition, which can facilitate learning, especially for regular worshipers. On the other hand, it's easy for formatting to make a specific form, and the entire worship experience, seem rote.

week, in same place in the service, at same time, and same station. There are so many creative options that provide much more depth of insight into God's activity than does a predictable approach. Dramatic forms are everywhere today—including in one's mind's eye—that have not yet been seen by the world. The drama of worship is in the encounter with God.

but who have gifts and callings to become a part of it. If the predictions are true and the world is going to become increasingly nonchurched, I muse that our attitudes about who to use and what to do in worship will shift, lest we miss the talents of the largest segment of America's population, the nonchurched non-Christian.

In most of today's megachurches, the "fringe" artist or gifted and perhaps called person who is just exploring Christianity would likely have a difficult time being recognized as a potential leader. Some megachurches might believe that only the most mature Christians should be in Christian leadership. Also, megachurches often see their worship formats themselves as missional, and many postmodern "fringe" artists would not fit into the established format because their art is too "edgy."

> I recently experienced a unique indigenous worship band at a denominational gathering. They weren't typical by any means. They weren't "beautiful" and they weren't young. They played praise and secular music from the 1960s and 1970s (e.g., "You've Got a Friend"). But they were authentic, the music was good, and they were fun. The table where I sat included many of the small number of Gen-X folks who attended this event, and they loved this band. I don't know how the band fares weekly in the local church, or how the worship affects the community, but maybe they're just quirky enough to be fabulous.

It's not the goal of the postmodern church to package the arts and make them predictable and formulaic. The heart of indigenous worship is the fluidity that comes from the mix occurring between that which is already present and that which is to come. There's unpredictability in that, but then, there's unpredictability any time a group of people gets together to create an artistic project.

Worship designers worry about doing the right thing, and sometimes they miss miracles as a result. A team developing something that grows out of the creativity of its community can have more power to reach out than the group or individual trying to find the exact style of music and order of worship to use in attracting the coveted nonchurched population that lives within walking distance from the church. The team's effort reaches out not only because it has heart, authenticity, and meaning, but also because it isn't prescribed. It's surprising.

> One might wonder if there is any way to measure what is "authentic" worship, when form and format aren't predictable. Is there anything that ties one worship experience to another? That question pushes me to further emphasize my belief that the measure of authentic worship isn't the form or format of the worship offering; rather, it's the touch of the Holy. When Jesus transforms one's soul in worship, one is pushed to radical action in the world, and finds himself or herself reaching out to others to offer them a brush with the touch that has radically changed this person's own life.

Leaders of postmodern worship teams push the envelope with regard to style, format, and the process of creativity, fostering an atmosphere of risk taking and openness to imperfection. Embracing change in worship by trying out new styles and forms, and by using the gifts and callings of those whom God delivers to your door belies the deeper value of trust in God to work through potential failure, as creativity often leads to experimentation. But if the focus of worship is on people and their struggle to know God in their own lives and cultural context, worship that's indigenous will go deep and wide, and will move beyond that which is known to be tried and true.

THE CALLED AND GIFTED

To get to the depth of indigenous worship, leaders need to think holistically about what it means to be called to and gifted for the ministry of worship design. Church leaders are being taught to develop teams of those who are called and gifted to accomplish a specific mission. With regard to worship design, that's a very layered picture. It's a play, within a play, within a play.

In one sense, all of us are called and gifted in worship. Those who sit in the pews or folding chairs are called to worship, and also gifted to worship. By God's creation, we design worship in the moments of worship, as we live our lives and as we sit, stand, and raise our arms in public worship each week. Congregational participants in worship are in your particular setting because of some connection they feel to the manner in which the gospel is presented through worship. And they affect the outcome of the worship because they're there, participating in what you do. In a sense, they're the second-largest segment of the worship design team.

The largest segment of the worship design team is those who aren't yet part of worship, be they unchurched or dechurched. In any church, there are always more who aren't there than are there. Yet, God is calling everyone to worship: "Go therefore and make disciples of all nations, baptizing them in the name of the Father and of the Son and of the Holy Spirit" (Matt. 28:19). And "at the name of Jesus every knee should bend, in heaven and on earth and under the earth, and every tongue should confess that Jesus Christ is Lord" (Phil. 2:9-10).

The nonchurched, non-Christian population whom the church exists to reach with the love of Christ helps design worship simply because it exists, and because public worship is as much for them as for the saints. For regular worshipers, the implications of the call to discipleship in worship are great. When worshiping congregations see themselves as called and gifted to worship, it changes how they understand the role of worship in community life. Worship becomes not something that is only between "me and God," but between "me, God, and others," as God uses "my" worship as a witness to the world.

The implications for the worship planning and worship leading teams are also great. They too must focus on the massive population who aren't yet in worship, making them more important to the process of worship design than their own assumptions, needs, desires, or abilities. It's an inverted approach to look at the real power lying not within the team of designers, but within the "lost and unsaved," or those who have never met the Holy God of Jesus face-to-face, but who are also called to and gifted for worship design according to God's creation.

Being called and gifted to be part of the team that plans or leads worship now takes on new meaning. In a sense, the artistic abilities of those called to the worship design team are less important than is their deep caring about the fate of the lives of those with whom they have no personal connection. Artistic abilities are not the end in themselves; rather, they are the venue through which team members articulate God's prevenient activity in the lives of all people in the community in which the church exists to serve God.

Most of us would think in terms of structuring our worship teams formulaically; to have a dancer, a musician, a director, a coordinator, an organizer, a teacher, a visionary. That's not wrong, and your team may wind up looking like that. However, "call" defines gifting, as gifting defines call. If a leader seeks those whom God has called to the worship ministry, he or she may realize the group's gifts do not match the leader's preconceived plan.

Those who are gifted and also called to worship design seek God's activity, and God seeks theirs. Each team member's unique gift and unique insight into what God is doing in every area of congregational life—which includes life outside the congregation—tap into God's plan for a particular community, when accompanied by God's call to be at the center of this fertile ministry.

Indigenous worship connects gifts, message, style, God's activities, and the hopes and dreams of the community, and much more. It is a ministry of passion that goes far and wide and deep and high, beyond the pages of this book. Indigenous experiences of the Holy touch the most profound places of God's presence in our lives.

Character Development: Improvisation

Improvisational theater, particularly comedy, amazes me. Actors make things up in the moment, and it's so relevant, you'd never know their dialogue wasn't scripted. Improv isn't always smooth, but even then, if the actors are good, the content is always meaningful and engaging.

Indigenous worship is also rather improvisational. It isn't scripted, and sometimes it's a little rough around the edges, because it happens in the moment, in culture, in the context of the spiritual journey. Just as improv contains lots of surprises for both the audience and the actors, indigenous worship is also surprising because it's homegrown. It fits.

HOT DISH

Some cultures make casseroles; Minnesotans make "hot dish." Regardless of its name, it's hash, any way you stir it. Likewise, there are similarities between blended worship and contemporary worship; only the name is different.

There has been much controversy about blended worship in the last several years. Some say that to blend worship is to ask for trouble, because you wind up offending everyone. But in truth, I can't think of any worship service I've attended that doesn't blend a variety of forms and style. Some of the forms that are introduced into contemporary worship are ancient, yet they fit so well that most don't realize how old they are. Helpful questions are: What can be blended and what can't be blended, and why? How can we think creatively about merging forms and styles to speak the truth?

ORIGINS

Most planning and leading teams offering indigenous worship write music, produce videos, choreograph drama-dances, or write dramas or liturgies. It goes with the territory, and should be encouraged. But not all churches will do all things. In 1999, Mike Slaughter, pastor of Ginghamsburg Church in Tipp City, Ohio, came to Minnesota to lead an event for my tribe. I asked him why his church didn't write music, with all the other original things they do there. He replied that God just hadn't led them to that yet.

ARRANGED MARRIAGES

There's a strange wedding between often unheard of or forgotten instruments to highly futuristic and electronic instruments in today's pop, rock, and even Christian music. Some of the new instrumentation is very old, if not ancient, and often ethnic, creating diversity of sound and expression. There are many possibilities for using innovative instrumentation to make well-known songs or even hymns sound new and different. Each original arrangement further identifies the indigenous worship of your community, and opens the door to higher involvement from the community.

QUIRKY

Over the years, I've worked with several adults who are learning disabled. I often formatted music differently for them than for the rest of the team so they could participate. This changed how the team operated together, enabling all to utilize the gifts and callings of others. Artists bring strange (and wonderful!) personality traits with them that leaders need to embrace. Worship teams operate as a body, and lift up the needs of others with collective strength. It's the glue of indigenous worship, experienced by the congregation.

STAGE DIRECTIONS

You may be thinking about taking a spiritual gift inventory to help you identify your spiritual gifts as articulated in 1 Corinthians 12; Romans 12; and Ephesians 4. I have taken two of them, and though they were both fun and informative, I also found them restrictive. There are times when God gives me a gift I didn't know I had because it didn't show up in the inventory. He asks me to use it for a time, and then takes it away when the usefulness has passed. Since it comes from God, I can't control its usage. I quarrel with Christians who say, "I have discernment; I have mercy." Sometimes it seems they consider it a badge of honor, as opposed to something that fits within a body of believers in order to enhance and inform the body of believers. As with other aspects of worship leading and planning, using gift inventories can become formulaic. Some leaders who work closely with their team can help a person see his or her own giftedness while encouraging openness to the movement of the Spirit, without having to use inventories. In the process, leaders encourage self-awareness in the participant, as well as model the process of being aware of spiritual gifts in others.

Read 1 Corinthians 12; Romans 12; and Ephesians 4

- What are some gifts Paul names that you don't understand? Discuss.
- What are some gifts you think God may have given you?
- What are some gifts you see in those in your team?
- What gifts do you wish you had? What gifts do you think would be beneficial to your team?
- Pray for God to reveal your gifts, and bring new gifts to your team.
- After completing the first five steps above, you may want to find a spiritual gifts inventory that you like, have all team members take it, and then talk about it.[2]

---

2. One inventory I've heard positive feedback from is called "LifeKeys." (For information, contact Changing Church, 200 E. Nicollet Boulevard, Burnsville, MN 55337.) There are many others to choose from. Several other organizations use "Network," which is Willow Creek's inventory. (For information, either go to <http://www.willowcreek.com/group.asp?action=l:s&groupid=53> or write to them at Willow Creek Community Church, 67 East Algonquin Road, South Barrington, IL 60010.)

IF YOU'RE STARTING A NEW SERVICE

1. Revisit the profile of your target constituency. Has it changed since you first developed it? What is new or different? What are you more sure of now?
2. What new clarity is God giving you about your mission, vision, and so forth?

WORSHIP TEAMS ARE AT THE HEART OF A LARGER ORGANISM

DIRECTOR'S NOTES

Every live drama is accomplished by the work of many teams. The actors would not be able to perform without the stagehands, the lighting and sound crews, the makeup artists, the artistic directors, and many more support teams. In the local church, thriving worship teams are central to an organic system of teams that beget more teams that work together to fulfill the church's mission.

DON AND MEREDITH

Don: *I keep wondering about what Pastor Connie said about Christendom being dead. Do you think she's just saying that because she wants to start a new worship service?*

Meredith: *It wouldn't surprise me. She's a manipulator. I've never heard Pastor John say anything like that. Sure, you see a lot of folks from different religions downtown and a lot of kids with the tattoos. But certainly, Christianity isn't dead.*

Don: *She didn't say Christianity is dead, Meredith, she said "Christendom." She means that you can't assume people are Christian anymore just because they're American.*

Meredith: Oh. Well anyway, look at how those kids dress and look. Christians don't do that.

Don: Jeremy says he's a Christian, and to look at him you probably wouldn't know it.

Meredith: He says he's a Christian, but he didn't have any idea what to do when he came to our church.

Don: Maybe his church just doesn't do what we do.

Meredith: I'm sure they don't! This worship book I read says certain things must be present before it's true worship. I really wonder if Jeremy's church is doing true worship, and if it's not true worship, then what is it?

Don: Well, he did seem a bit disengaged when he came with Jen, but I don't know if we can assume the worst. The truth is, Meredith, Pastor Connie is right. There aren't a lot of young people in our worship service.

Meredith: And she says it's because they can't relate, which is exactly what I just said. They don't have a good enough background in worship.

Don: Do you think they all went to church as children?

Meredith: Of course they did. Most of them did, I'm sure. Maybe not the kids from the bad families. But most of them probably went to church as children.

Don: I think Pastor Connie is saying that a lot of them probably didn't.

Meredith: That's the most ridiculous thing I've ever heard. And there are young people who come to our church. Is she blind?

Don: *Yes, we do have some young people, but not as many as we used to. And Jen is one of them who isn't here anymore.*

Meredith: *That's what I'm worried about. She'd rather go with Jeremy.*

Don: *It can't be that bad for her, can it? Jeremy seems to be interested in Jesus.*

Meredith: *What if he's some kind of radical fundamentalist?*

Don: *Well, he didn't really seem that way to me.*

Meredith: *Have you ever heard Pastor John talk about Jesus like that?*

Don: *Pastor John talks about Christ.*

Meredith: *See what I mean? Only fundies get carried away with "Jesus this," and "Jesus that."*

Don: *I know. It's offensive. It makes me feel very uncomfortable.*

Meredith: *The young people who come here say they like what we do because it's familiar. They like singing hymns and they don't like loud music. And these young people are bringing their children to our church . . .*

Don: *But do you think Pastor Connie wants young people like the ones that are already here? I got the impression she wants people like Jeremy.*

Meredith: *Those people will ruin our church.*

Don: *And it will be her fault.*

Meredith: *Don, it won't be long until there will be nothing left of our heritage, or our building. It's as though she wants to kick us out. We're in our mid-fifties, Don.*

Don: *Well if what you say is true, Meri, about there being a right way and a wrong way to worship, then we need to have Pastor Connie read that book.*

Meredith: *She did read it, and she didn't like it. A famous expert on worship wrote this book, Don. I'd like to know what books Pastor Connie has written about worship.*

Don: *You should give that book to the worship committee to read. That would give them some ammunition to withhold the money they need to start that service.*

Meredith: *Yes, that would be good. I think she's just jealous because she's not the senior pastor. We should give the book to Pastor John too. He'll straighten her out.*

Most of us have a temptation to latch onto an organizational structure as though it were a lifeline. Though we need structure to organize our ministries, we're often so enamored of the "ministry model" that we project upon it all of our hopes and dreams to grow our churches large, and expect it to bring immediate success. In the process, we obscure the deeper soul work that is really at the root of lasting change.

> I grew up in an addictive environment, and I know how difficult it is to change the habits that addictions bring. An individual can make great strides toward health, then one day awaken and realize he's stumbled into yet another addictive environment.

In the Christendom church, pastors and church leaders create elaborate structures and models for their ministries, and lay them out like a template on a group of people called the church, with each job in the church being a cutout where a warm body can slip in to fulfill a function. Everyone expects the template to define their character by giving them each a job to do. It's mechanical and very subtle, but oh so powerful: fill a slot, go to a meeting, fill a slot, go to a meeting, fill a slot, go to a meeting.

The power of the template is like a drug, and drug usage causes addiction. If you look at the people who are addicted to the machinery of the church, you find their eyes either blank and dull, or you find them complaining about going to meetings while simultaneously hearing in their voices how thrilled they are to be involved in the busyness of so many decision-making groups.[1]

To develop a successful worship arts ministry that endures in today's world and is able to bring lasting change into both the church environment and people's lives, you will need a strong infrastructure. However, there is a difference between the way an organism operates and the way a machine operates. If you're going to develop a worship arts ministry that can bring radical transformation in today's world, you have to think of it as an organism rather than a machine, or it won't survive.

> Some church leaders have read all the material that's out there today and know the rhetoric concerning the need for teams and organic structures. So they create an elaborate template for their church, they call it a team structure, and they have cutouts in the template where the warm bodies go to fill a slot. Because it's called a team structure, it's believed to be organic, when it's nothing more than a traditional structure in disguise.

---

1. Thomas Bandy is the first person I heard talk about addiction to the Christendom machine. I have worked in addictive church environments, but I never was able to put my finger on why they were addictive. I knew they were addictive only because as I observed my own behavior, I saw that it was becoming a throwback to days of yore. Though I had worked hard to grow and become healthy, I found myself behaving in ways that were all too familiar. When I heard Tom talk about the addiction to the machinery, I recognized the connection instantly. It was a watershed moment. Addiction of any kind is seductive.

Addressing the mechanical model of the Christendom church is challenging. The mechanical model is ingrained into anyone in ministry today who grew up in the church. Even younger pastors of brand-new churches battle tendencies toward creating mechanical infrastructures. The mechanical infrastructure is second nature to even the most forward-thinking individuals and has to be recognized and unlearned. And that's very hard to do, because those in the midst of ministry shaped according to the Christendom mechanical model are so tired from doing church the Christendom way that to think of doing it differently is overwhelming, even if they realize change will be ultimately positive. Also, most of us don't believe that the machine is really that powerful that it actually will have an effect on the worship. Our disbelief helps us deny how attached we are to the model itself.

If you plan worship before you understand your genetic code, your worship has great potential to become prescribed, since you'll most likely be copying something you've seen elsewhere without thinking what it means to be indigenous. That's a mechanical approach. Or, if you try to develop an organic structure for your church to support your worship arts ministry without thinking about the impact of change upon the mechanical structure, you will sabotage your efforts, because the Christendom model is not set up to handle change. The Christendom model will try to eradicate any notion of trying something new—like a worship service or a new team structure—because it radically upsets the balance of the system. If you as a leader are not prepared to face the conflict brought into the system by introducing change into it, it's the same as saying you don't want to change.

It's a waste of everyone's time to start a new worship service or attempt a team approach to planning an existing service without looking toward systemic change. Starting new worship or changing worship in an established environment is like doing an organ transplant without treating the system with antirejection medicine. The new worship is a foreign body that can only be accepted with a view toward systemic change.

Dealing with denial is essential to overcoming addiction. Several years ago, I went to the hospital to see a family member, a chronic alcoholic, who was suffering from cirrhosis. I hadn't seen her in months and I burst into tears to see this beautiful, intelligent woman who had become unrecognizable. She said, "Cathy, you need to know, this isn't all from alcohol." She died two weeks later. Likewise, church leaders may wonder why their churches are bleeding and dying. If it isn't the destructive impact of their drug of choice—the mechanical model—upon the natural body system of the local church that is causing the church's vital organs to fail, what is it?

In the church, systemic change is not a top-down process, rather it is bottom up. Leaders and worship teams who are the first to recognize the need for change need to grasp the whole picture of systems in the church to be able to see where the bottom actually is before embarking on a crusade to make things different. If, in a mechanical system, change is not carefully thought through and led with deep conviction, one could have disastrous results.

Change begins when a person sees the natural body system of the church as a living, breathing organism—the Body of Christ—that exists to bring Jesus into the world. It exists to make disciples who, in turn, make more disciples who believe that the world can be changed because of the love of God in Jesus Christ. The church does not exist for itself. It is not a building or an entity that is defined by its size or its structure. It is a living, breathing body that is an extension of the arms, legs, hands, feet, mind, soul, thoughts, and feelings of Jesus Christ. There is no other purpose for the church than that. It must be free to grow and spread in order to fulfill its destiny.

An infrastructure that honors the organic nature of the church is one that offers the organism the freedom to grow and be what it is. It does not control any activity of the organism as long as the organism is fulfilling its destiny. The infrastructure is not egotistical and has no need to be recognized for itself; rather it is a part of the natural DNA of the organism known as a body of believers.

The infrastructure of such an organism is team based. Teams are mission driven, and have no need for self-fulfillment, or a need to control or be controlled by a hierarchy, since the entire organism lives to fulfill the same mission and understands its purpose according to the same values and beliefs.

Postmodern worship thrives in such a system. In healthy, organically organized bodies of believers, worship and outreach are central to the mission of the church. No threat exists when a new worship service begins because the worship grows out of the genetic code of the organism, and all parts of the organism exist to fulfill the same mission.

In our institutionally alienated world, the mechanical template is anathema to potential postmodern worshipers, because it exists for it's own recognition, as opposed to existing to fulfill the mission of the church. This template demands attention and allegiance, and begins to take over the body and destroy the natural infrastructure that supports and encourages the destiny of the body of believers.

Your mission as a leader in your local church is to become a part of the natural infrastructure of the organism, so that the organism is free to be what it is, nothing more and nothing less. Surprisingly, in a system that is controlled by a mechanical model, becoming part of the natural infrastructure of an organic ministry means not focusing on the mechanical structure. The paradox is that the healing of the system begins when you first try to change yourself.

RAISING THE BOTTOM

To use a metaphor from chemical dependency treatment, when someone focuses on "self" as a way to begin the process of change, it's like raising the bottom for others who are part of the addictive system. All addicts have to "hit bottom" in order to recover. There has to be a very important reason for any addict to give up the source of his or her addiction. But focusing on the addict only causes denial. Instead, if one person who is important enough to the addict changes his or her own life, it causes extreme discomfort for the addict and thus creates an opening for the entire addictive system to change. In effect, the bottom is raised up so that the addict hits it sooner than if left to his or her own devices.

A pastor or other church leader could be important enough in the life of the church to disrupt the system of addiction that prevails in the body, if and when he or she begins to change his or her leadership style. Think of the addicted church as a mobile, which revolves in delicate balance around a (mechanical) superstructure that joins all the parts. The parts are all connected yet disengaged. If one part—a pastor or church leader—becomes disconnected from the mobile by becoming engaged in mission, and thus changes the way he or she operates within the system, you can easily see what would happen. The functioning of the entire system would be disrupted.

> The mechanical environment is very pastor focused. Pastor is hero, enabling the community to believe there's nothing wrong; pastor is scapegoat, enabling the community to point to him or her as the cause of all the problems; pastor is employee, letting everyone tell him or her what to do. Many pastors love their roles, enjoying the focus that the congregation gives to them; others don't realize they're receiving negative attention. Still others see themselves as part of the problem, yet don't believe there's any other way.

The balance of the mobile in a mechanical church is the same as it is in any other addictive system. The church revolves around a mechanical superstructure in perfect balance, connected by the mechanism and disengaged from real depth in transformational ministry. When a person or group of people of great importance to the system either change or leave the system, the system has to fight to maintain balance. The system will either find someone to replace the one who changed, or it will pull the changed person or group back into the addictive patterns so that everything can return to normal and the system can continue revolving around the mechanical superstructure.

Or the system itself can change, which takes leadership. This is not the "traditional" type of leadership; it's not "top-down," or a demand for change. It's an inverted brand of leadership that begins with self-change by someone in the system who is important enough to make a difference, whose lack of presence will throw the mobile out of balance. The pastor or another leader is such a person.[2] If the pastor or key leader is able to recognize the need for change, and begin the process by changing his or her leadership style and ultimately his or her heart and soul, real change can begin. Self-change leads pastors to engage a disengaged congregation by changing attitudes among the body. Slowly, new and organic systems develop; ultimately, organizational change occurs.

Of course, that explanation sounds easier than it is. Self-change is painful. Further, it's even more painful when the system tries to pull the leader back so that the system doesn't have to change. Leaders are very tempted to let go of their new directions and avoid dealing with the power of the machinery, even if they desperately seek transformational change.

In order to ultimately affect system-wide change, leaders can't change for any other reason than to honor their own relationship with God. Changing oneself or thinking about leaving the system in order to fix the system is not desirable, because there are no guarantees the system will change. Trying to fix the

---

2. As I mentioned briefly in Act 1, Dick Wills had a very clear vision from God for his life while he was on retreat from his duties as lead pastor. After the retreat, he went to his church and told them about the vision. He told them he would follow the vision there, at Christ Church, or elsewhere, but that following the vision was nonnegotiable.

system is to control the system. And leading systemic change is not about control, it's about surrender to God, his will, and his desire for hope and fulfillment. To be able to lead systemic change requires faith, clear mission, and the drive to follow God's leading at all cost. Systemic change occurs by the grace of God.

Character Development: Black Comedy

Comedies about death aren't for everyone. In fact, they can be downright offensive. But I've always rather enjoyed dark comedies, finding in them much irony and truth to challenge my assumptions.

> Most church leaders don't realize just how deeply into change a new worship service will take them, since they think of the new service as just another cutout in the template.

The process of systemic change is a bit of a black comedy. It involves death—the death of old, destructive patterns, and ironic humor—that others change best when you leave them alone. Many twists of truth emerge in the process of systemic change.

Bottom-up systemic change is not quick; it's a long process. It helps to approach it with wit and grace.

ROLE REVERSAL: MECHANICAL TEMPLATE DEFINES
HUMAN BEINGS

Earlier in this book, I asked the reader to contemplate the importance of worship in his or her life and the life of the community. I now raise the question again. For worship changes to succeed, the body must value worship above all else. Worship defines humans, not a mechanical structure. Worship and evangelism are the lifeblood of churches that reach nonbelievers with the truth of the gospel.

ISN'T IT IRONIC?

A new worship service can be like an intervention as it is a good tool for leveraging change in a mechanically organized church. If the new worship service is used to help the community focus on topics like genetic code or indigenous worship, and it helps the community see the need for change, it becomes part of the process of raising the bottom. Instead of sweeping the anxiety of the community under the carpet, leaders can use the new service to help the congregation see what God is up to as members murmur and resist the move toward the future.

ACROPASTOR

Imagine a person with a toothy grin, wearing a black suit and a clerical collar while doing the splits between two chairs. One chair is labeled "mechanical structure," and the other is labeled, "organic structure."

When pastors and worship teams see the need for change, they want it yesterday. Leaders make the mistake of trying to

---

A client of mine says that his appointment to his new church was a leverage point for change. He's the first new pastor in twenty-five years to paint a picture of transformation, which has led to an increase of 65 percent in worship attendance and $10,000 in giving in less than a year. He has been coaching a team to start a new worship service and he's been trying to escape the committee mentality and move visionaries into financial leadership. These are the only "concrete" changes he's aiming for until attitudes shift, though he believes he has only a small window of time to ride the tide of energy brought by his presence and new vision. The new system is emerging and the old one is slowly dying. He's in two places at once, and it's nearly insane. And he always says life couldn't be any better.

---

restructure the church too early in the process, knowing that the new structure will support the new service better than the mechanical structure will. The problem with that theory is that organizational change won't last unless attitudes have changed. That's why this type of leadership is an inverted approach, or bottom up. Attitudinal change precedes organizational change.

Systemic change is very demanding, since pastors wind up operating in two systems at once. As the lead pastor changes and then leads attitudinal change, and as new systems begin to develop, the old system doesn't automatically stop. Full organizational change happens last, much after systemic change has begun, and long after many have begun a deep and gradual journey of transformation. Pastors need to limber up, as systemic change feels a lot like doing the splits.

THEATER OF THE ABSURD

It seems absurd when one plays the part of a servant in a world that understands taking, not giving; power, not submission.

At some point, the lead pastor needs to develop a core leadership team whose job it will be to lead a servant-empowering organism. The core leaders are a different group from the worship team. Gathering and developing the core leadership team is much the same process as gathering and developing the worship team. The core leadership team is handpicked and infused with the DNA, and turned loose to continue building the teams that are comprised within the organism.[3]

One caveat: keep it simple. An organism isn't cumbersome. It may be intricate, with many branches that intertwine and connect the different offshoots to one another, but it is consistent within itself, and thereby uncomplicated. The organism of the church is team; the worship team is at the heart of such an organism.

---

3. See Thomas G. Bandy's *Christian Chaos: Revolutionizing the Congregation* (Nashville: Abingdon, 1999) to learn about the organic structure of the servant-empowering organization.

KNOWING WHEN IT'S TIME TO CHANGE

When is it time to finally make the shift from a mechanical structure to a fully organic system? No matter what aspect of change you're embracing, knowing when to make your move centers on God's timing, not on completing a checklist of tasks. Sometimes you know in your heart that God is ready, even though it seems like there is still so much to do. Other times, though there seems to be a lot in place, God is telling you to wait. Leaders of change look for signs that point to the readiness of the team and the community to go to the next step in becoming a servant-empowered organism.

WAITING

Teams that are ready to change are ready to wait on God. Waiting is fertile godly time. He's doing something in you and in the community when you are willing to wait to hear his voice. Because oftentimes those who aren't ready to wait for God will rise up against leaders, waiting can sometimes seem like persecution. When a leadership team or community is able to withstand the pressure and trust the waiting time, it's a sign of spiritual maturity.

GRIEVING

The community will need to grieve the loss of the familiar. Leaders of change will recognize and even encourage grieving for and openness to the emotional journey of systemic and organizational change.

ACCEPTING

Grieving leads one to accept the many losses that accompany change. But some will not grieve and will not be able to accept the loss of their favorite mechanical structure. They will be angry and defensive, and will seek another mechanical system, since the one in which they found their source of sameness has vanished. Healthy leadership teams will not try to stop the departure of the addicted, and will instead pray for their eventual transformation.

149

CHOOSING

Teams make a tactical error thinking there's only one way to start a new service or restructure an old one. Spiritual maturity can be measured to some extent in one's ability to consider all the possibilities for moving ahead, even when the options seem outlandish. God works through options.

DISCIPLINING

Teams that are practicing spiritual disciplines of prayer, fasting, study, and tithing are showing signs of maturity and readiness for moving forward. The ability to confess personal and team shortcomings is also a sign of spiritual maturity. Mature teams are bonded in truth.

AMASSING

Starting a new worship service requires critical mass. By this I mean that you have to have enough people present in the worship space so that a newcomer doesn't feel "on display" or threatened in any way. Systemic change also requires critical mass. There have to be enough people in the community who are supportive of the idea of restructuring for it to be successful. Critical mass is one of the concrete signs that it's time to make a move.[4]

DEPARTING

Systemic change is demanding. Sometimes the leader needs to say, "Enough." When there is no possibility that leadership can fulfill personal mission and the call to discipleship, it's time to move on.

---

4. Critical mass is a combination of committed disciples and new Christians who are invited to be a part of a new worship ministry. Leaders establish critical mass prior to the launch date of public worship so that there are enough people in the designated worship space to make it feel full and so that a newcomer won't feel awkward. Some churches try to start public worship with a critical mass of two hundred people. Others begin very small, and set goals to increase numbers as they go. When starting a second service in an established congregation, some suggest as few as fifty people to begin. Details of critical mass are contextual.

STAGE DIRECTIONS

Share stories of individual and corporate journeys.

- What are some of the strengths of your team thus far?
- What are your growth areas?
- What kind of reaction has the discussion of systemic change triggered in the team?

HOW CONNECTED ARE YOUR TEAMS?

Regarding worship teams specifically, have you yet considered how you'll organize your teams? Earlier, in the chapter entitled "How to Wrestle with This Octopus," I offered some suggestions for worship-team structure. Revisit that section, then consider the following questions:

- How is your design team organized?
- Who is on the worship-leading team?
- What additional teams might be effective within your specific context?

IF YOU'RE STARTING A NEW SERVICE

Earlier in this book, I suggested starting worship as a small community, which is one way to build critical mass prior to the launch date. Consider the following questions:

- Do you have possible future launch dates for beginning public worship?
- What has yet to be put in place?
- What's already in place?
- Do you have a flexible timeline in place that will help the community prepare, but yet not restrict God's surprises?
- What are the implications of your new service for the greater community, and how will you and your team deal with those?

WORSHIP TEAMS CHANGE LIFE

DIRECTOR'S NOTES

It's not possible to write about or portray a character without being changed by what you have written or portrayed. It opens you to new ways of looking at the world, because you're seeing the world from someone else's point of view. Watching or participating in a drama—be it a drama of the legitimate stage or a worship offering—can change you in the same way, thereby changing the way you interact with the world around you. Dramas have the power to change the world for good or for ill.

PASTOR JOHN

These are strange times we live in. I never thought I'd see the day when I was faced with the kind of changes in the church that we are being faced with today. I don't think I can keep up.

Connie is such a dynamo. I just wish she'd leave me alone. I don't see why she just doesn't do what she wants to with that service without involving me. I give her plenty of freedom, but she still keeps pushing me. Drives me crazy.

It really doesn't help me when people like Don and Meredith come to me with their books about worship and their negative feelings about Connie. I can see why they don't like her. She threatens them. Heck, she threatens me. I wish they wouldn't come to me with all their complaints, though. I have enough headaches.

But I have to listen to them and let them spew. I guess that's my role. And they certainly mean well, and are only trying to protect their investments. The worship committee is dead set against Connie and

*her worship ideas too. So is the choir. I wish they'd all just go straight
to Connie and tell her themselves. But I get stuck doing it all the time
because they never do. And Connie has a right to know what people
are saying about her. She gets so mad at me when I tell her what people are talking about behind her back. But she needs to know..*

*I don't think Connie realizes what she's dealing with sometimes.
Don and Meredith are two of the biggest givers we have. And
they're very well connected. They're charter members; they know
virtually everyone. Connie can't possibly think it's a good idea to
alienate them like she does.*

*Frankly, I think she's dreaming if she thinks some of those rebel-
lious kids that she's trying to attract from outside the church will
ever find their way into a church. She is wasting her time.*

*She told me the other day that I need to change, that it's my job to
change. Well, maybe she's right. Maybe I do need to change. But what
would that mean? Sometimes I think I'll never be a good leader, so
why would I ever bother trying to change? Besides, I don't have time.
I look at the pile of papers on my desk and I feel buried. I think about
all the meetings I need to attend and I just want to go take a nap.*

*Connie is so demanding sometimes. And she's got tunnel vision.
At the rate she's going, she'll get herself booted out of here. Maybe
that's a good idea—let her go ruffle someone else's feathers. In the
meantime, I'm just going to stay out of her way. I'm going to retire
in a few years anyway.*

True love brings extraordinary change. For those of us who
have received the love of Jesus, we know that truth firsthand.
I'm a completely different person since I've known Jesus from
the person I was before he came into my life. God continues to
soften the hard edges of my own heart. His love has shown me
patience, peace, and trust, and I'm open to whatever he chooses
to reveal to me about myself, so that I can grow closer to him.

Seeing the truth about ourselves is our "life mission," should
we choose to accept it. If people are to grow in their lives, they
need to give up the things that cause them to be "stuck" in their
anger, apathy, prejudice, rebelliousness, or self-blame. Many
people don't want to change, or don't see that they need to

change. I think it may be because they don't have a savior, and haven't known extraordinary love. I think it's because they don't really know what is possible.

To truly grow as human beings, we need to be authentically aware of whom we are, broken and lost. That's impossible for human beings to do without the kind of enduring love that we receive from Jesus. When I think of the way I was before I knew Jesus, I know that I could not have changed without him. When I compare myself now to the way I was before, I am amazed that I could change as much as I have. But this change didn't come about from anything I did. Jesus, in me, has made me new.

Some say they have Jesus in their lives, yet we don't see the change in them that his extraordinary love brings. I wonder why that is. I speculate that it's either because they haven't received his love as it was intended, or they haven't shared it. If they haven't shared it, then do they really have it and know it as it was intended?

In August 2000, Bill Clinton appeared at Willow Creek's Leadership Summit Conference, confessing his sinfulness with Monica Lewinsky to more than four thousand pastors and to the nation who watched the event televised on *Nightline*. Many pastors were angry with Bill Hybels, senior pastor at Willow Creek, for offering forgiveness. They doubted Clinton's sincerity, citing the language and setting as inappropriate. Scathing comments about both Hybels and Clinton flourished among clergy and churchgoers. Truly, it's hard to think of anyone more politically astute than Bill Clinton. Many cited the timing of his appearance at Willow Creek as questionable because of its proximity to the Democratic National Convention. However, I'm more struck by the quickness with which the body concludes that anyone should or shouldn't be forgiven. In Christendom, such judgment over life issues is common, keeping many people out of the church.

When human beings know the love of God that leads to self-awareness even in the midst of the sad truth about how unlovely we are, God asks us to share it with another human being so that he can be revealed again and again. He asks us to love the unlovely, and to show patience, peace, and trust to the frustrating, angry, and untrustworthy. God has shown that to me after all, even though I have not deserved any of it. It's the seed of transformation.

But though I have (somewhat laboriously) received his eternal love, to give it away has been at least as great a challenge (if not an even greater one) as letting go of my own pride so that I could accept my own sins. God has continued to love me through all my foibles, and I've continued to offer judgment or condemnation to others for theirs. I've decided that I must not really have received God's love if I haven't given it away.

It has taken years of God loving me for me to look at others with the eyes of God. I am not perfect at it by any means, but I have noticed that little by little, I'm doing just that. True love brings extraordinary change.

In the preceding pages, I've talked about many things that define worship designers. But above all else, it's God's love that defines us. Without it, nothing else matters. Worship designers exist to reveal God's love to the world, and they do it through their worship of God. Team life is an aspect of worship. Being part of a worship design team that follows the journey of transformation literally changes life, since to live and breathe worship design together means to offer continuous love. Teams would not survive without it.

LOVE OF TEAM

Working within a team is an experience of community, and community is an experience of both joy and conflict. The greatest gift a team brings is the openness to clash, because in the clashing, God takes hold. Sometimes the clashing is interpersonal; sometimes it's intrapersonal.

In working closely in teams, so many things come up that

concern one's personal life issues. In the midst of team, we seek control, recognition, power, and affirmation. At the same time, we're arrogant, dominating, self-centered, and shallow. (I jokingly say that team brings out the best in people!) All those things need to be confronted, lest they insidiously eat away at the fiber of who God is calling us to be.

> Many times, leaders will say, "Our worship has gotten dull and rote, and we need someone to help us figure out some things to do to become more lively." My first thought is usually, "I wonder what is going on in the team?" Often, if a team is planning worship and the worship has become dull and lifeless, it's because the team's members have plateaued in their relationships, and have avoided the conflict that contains in it the potential for spiritual depth. Conflict offers endless opportunities for growth in thought or behavior, and can be fertile ground for God to plant these new seeds of opportunity, and should therefore be embraced, not avoided.

People have a tendency to fear truth telling. So then, what are the alternatives? Harmful silence? Placating? Codependence? Hatred? If we avoid the conflict that always comes up in the midst of team, we become bland or bitter. We allow someone's arrogance to run rampant, or someone's need for affirmation to obscure the inadequacy of what they've offered to God in worship. It's false and mechanical, and it leads to worship that is also false and mechanical.

Worshiping Jesus is worshiping the God of truth. We stand side by side with other sinners who are fully human, some of whom recognize that they need Jesus to give them what they can't possibly get on their own, others of whom have no idea that they can't master life themselves. At the center of the vocational worship designer's work is the recognition of his or her own need for God's truth, and the awareness of the diverse levels of recognition other worshipers have for their own need for God's truth.

But God's truth isn't sledgehammer- or baseball bat-truth. Sometimes humans receive truth that way, and sometimes we can't hear the truth any other way. Yet with God, truth is love. It's "love, love, love, extraordinary love." You can't separate God's truth from his love. Knowing God's truth about ourselves also shows his love. And if we think we know the truth and don't feel the love, then we don't know God's truth. Worship is about God's truth wrapped in love.

The most valuable lesson I learned in working in teams is that I need to accept others for exactly who they are, the entire imperfect package. I need to look at those with whom I partner with great love, through the eyes of God. I can do so because I have been looking at myself with those eyes. The paradox is that the love behind my eyes, which leads to total acceptance, is exactly what enables me to be truthful and exactly what leads to change, with others and myself. It's painful too, but so very rich.

Everything I've discussed in the pages of this book is about love. God's clarity, the awareness of how he interacts in worship, the way he interacts in culture, the way we are led to design worship that speaks to our own lives, the way we are led to change an entire system because of working this way—all of these have at their roots God's extraordinary love. Or, stating this another way: worship designers should have as their goal God's love in every aspect of what they do. All roads lead to love.

The goal of twenty-first-century worship designers is to work so closely with one another and with God that they are able to continue going deeper, wider, higher, and longer than they could have gone alone. Twenty-first-century worship designers love to love, and allow the Holy Spirit to take them ever further in their journeys—through their conflict and fights—with sustenance.

When the team continues to return to worship design with love—both interpersonally and corporately—it seeps into the daily lives of the worship designers, and into the worship that they design. Others feel it and are attracted to it, and so it affects the community who comes to see what all the fuss is about. Further, it seeps into the life of the church, and challenges the complacency and apathy that infiltrates the ethos of many congregations.

CORPORATE LOVE

It's risky to finally allow the true transformational love of Jesus to begin surfacing in any congregation that hasn't really been open to it before. Though Jesus' love is always there and never leaves us regardless of what we do, it does ask something of us. It asks us to receive it, and many of us don't. We fight it. As I've said, for a human being to receive the authentic love of Christ, it takes openness and authenticity about one's own hardness of heart, and an equal openness to accepting the hard hearts of others. Instead, many of us greet God with more hardness, defensiveness, and resistance, and greet one another with anger and rage.

> I've heard of a few church leaders who have received death threats because they introduced the real Jesus into the life of the congregation. Others have gotten emotionally beat up by those refusing to let the scales fall from their eyes. Ministry is dangerous work.

But taking the risk with Jesus' love is inevitable if you're developing twenty-first-century worship designers who are really responding to God's love. The love they find will be released in the worship they design, in the way they interact with one another, in the way they treat their primary relationships, and in the greater community. It isn't possible for it not to seep out. There is also no question in my mind that when it does come out, and a congregation is faced with the transformational love of Jesus for the first time, they will resist it. Everyone resists it at first because it's so very powerful.

When they resist, the answer is to offer "love, love, love, extraordinary love." It takes a long time to change a congregation and a human heart with love, and it takes a lot of love to

158

do it. It takes the eyes of love, and the openness to see Jesus in another human being. If I look at a congregation through my own fear, disdain, or addictions, I will see just that. But if I look at others with the eyes of God—though others are obviously frightened, disdainful, or addicted—I will still see God's hope, and the potential in the power of the Resurrection.

And I will be able to say what I see. I will be able to say that I see the fears, disdain, and addictions of others because I see them in myself. And because I have God's love, that makes it somehow okay to be exactly who I am, just as God's love makes it okay for you to be exactly who you are. The power of the Resurrection is in my self-acceptance, in spite of myself, and my self-acceptance, in turn, leads me to receive others in the same way. Acceptance is truth in love, and that leads to change.

But for leaders who love Jesus and who seek the power of his transformation, there is a price. Most of us who have led teams, congregations, and one another into this holy place that is so filled with darkness find ourselves enduring the "dark night of the soul." Some leaders never make it; some get sick; some get terribly discouraged; some get "shrewish"; some leave a congregation in favor of greener pastures that maybe are less demanding and are filled with those who can see with the eyes of God.

But I would say that every community, regardless of how open to change it seems, has its challenges, and has in it eyes that know no love. Further, I would rather have months of dark nights and an anguished soul than to be empty and hard in my own heart. I'd rather take on the love of Jesus and attempt to share it in any community than not. I'd rather live than die, therefore, I'd die to live.

There was a time in my ministry that I was angered to have to face the dark night of the soul. In my personal life and professional life I fought it. It has been some time since I've had to endure the feeling of hopelessness. I'd hate to say that it's because I've changed, lest I become arrogant. I'd hate to say that I don't expect to ever feel hopeless again. I don't know that. But, I have now known hope, and it has changed the way I look at the world.

Community Love

I have definitely become more optimistic as I've grown in faith. When I first started in professional ministry, I didn't think I could tell people the truth. I thought I had to manipulate change. At my first church, we changed the worship format from traditional to contemporary. We changed it very quickly, without any of the passion of adoring God, or of sharing love that would lead to the change of heart that I now know it can. We did it that way to get our way. Though ultimately the service was a success, many people were hurt by these changes and left the church.

There was another way, and that way would have been to speak in great love to people who I believe had lost their passion, or maybe had never had passion in the first place. Many people responded to our changes by exerting control and showing anger over what we were doing, and I can't really blame them. Had we followed the path of change with love at its center, I believe we'd have discipled people instead of disregarding them. I believe in the power of God's love. God could have discipled those people, but our control didn't allow it.

By rushing to change the worship, we lost not only the hearts of those who left or stayed in anger, but also the hearts of those with whom that group would potentially interact, those who were not a part of that or any congregation, but a part of God's world and desperately in need of God's love. Now, who will love them? As I recall the sea of faces of our congregation during that transition time, I know that many of the people who resisted change would likely have come along if we who were leading the change had not ourselves resisted; for we resisted God by moving too fast.[1] In truth, we were just as afraid as they were, it simply took a different form.

---

1. Church leaders often think and act to an extreme, believing they have much more or much less time than they actually have to lead change. You can't wait too long, or you'll become ingrown, but you can't push too fast, or you'll lose trust. Leading change is an art that involves listening, timing, and courage, among other things.

> When members of the congregation begin to share the love of Jesus outside the church walls, you know that they are seeing themselves as part of the worship team, and are living to fulfill a godly mission and lead transformation.

The whole point of change in worship that looks toward systemic change is to change hearts. The whole point of change in the church is to bring God's love into the world. When these are our goals and our focus, I believe that people will not only follow, but will actually begin to lead.

God has said, "Every knee should bend . . . and every tongue confess that Jesus Christ is Lord" (Phil. 2:10-11). Everyone in God's world is called to worship; it is the love that he offers us that finally brings us to our knees. We in the church need to be at the center of offering that love into the world. We worship God's love into being.

Character Development: The Star of the Show

Actors worry about who will get top billing because the biggest name means bigger fame and bigger purses. Silver and gold don't interest Jesus. He's interested in the treasures of heaven. If there is a star in this show, it's love, which seeks not fame or fortune, but a tender heart. That is the message of eternity, of what is, what was, and what is to come.

INSIGHT

Great leaders are self-reflective. They will set up accountability systems for themselves so that parishioners and colleagues can be truthful with them when they've forgotten their humanity. Self-reflection is love. If you know Jesus and understand that you're accepted in his love just as you are, it frees you to be human and err, to confess with openness, and to know that others are human and need the same freedom that Jesus has given you.

HINDSIGHT

Self-reflection requires forgiveness. Without it, it's more like self-destruction. In a sense, forgiveness of self is hindsight; we see what has happened in the past and use it to understand the future.

FORESIGHT

Forgiveness doesn't mean letting go of your vision, mission, beliefs, and values. In fact, it's quite the opposite. I don't think you can have true compassion without knowing exactly what you stand for and why you're doing what you're doing. You can't speak the truth even with love unless you truly understand your own foundation. Love doesn't mean allowing a person or a system to manipulate you out of following your mission, and mercy doesn't mean forgetting the path you're on in order to offer someone understanding. True compassion happens in the midst of clarity and focus. Love happens in the midst of following the path you're on in utter faith.

STAGE DIRECTIONS

There is a song on one of my CDs called "I Will Give." It's about the challenge that most of us face when giving our hearts and souls completely to God. We may wish to give our hearts to God, but it's so much easier to remain stuck in the familiar aspects of our hopelessness and sin, even if we don't like those parts of ourselves.

The words of the song can be a point of discussion for your team. Words to songs without the music are sometimes incomplete, since the tune can influence the meaning of the lyrics. Still, perhaps your team members can spend some time thinking about the lyrics below, and then sharing their reactions with one another. Or, you may find a different song that would have more meaning to you.

Think about these and other questions:

• Where do you think God wants to take you next?
• How is God's love beginning to open your heart a little more?
• What are some walls of resistance to God's movement?

IF YOU'RE STARTING A NEW SERVICE

How well has your "private" worship evolved to this point? Are you inviting others into your community so that it's less private?

I Will Give

I will give my hand to you, if I can let it go
For my hand is a part of me, and I'm used to it O Lord
I will give my shame to you, if I can let it go
For my shame is a part of me, and I'm used to it O Lord

I can see you on the cross, with the nails in your hands and feet
And you know that I'm feeling lost, cause your compassion, it
   pierces me
And you know all the pain I feel, and you know that my pain is
   real
I will give you all of me, if your compassion will set me free

I will give my heart to you, if I can let it go
For my heart is a part of me, and I'm used to it, O Lord

I will give myself to you, if I can let it go
For my self is a part of me, and I'm used to it, O Lord[2]

---

2. Cathy Townley, "I Will Give," © WellSprings Unlimited, 1999. The song can be found on the WellSprings CD *Sing Your Praises*, and can be ordered through <www.wellsprings.org> or <www.easumbandy.com>.

SOLILOQUY

What Does It Mean When You Fall in Love?
by Susan A.

What does it mean
When you fall in love?
Does it mean
That life will be different now?
Will I be happy? Satisfied?
Is there a good future
To see,
For a change?

Anyway, I'm sure I wouldn't know.
Has there ever been love for me?
I've wanted it, desperately.
But no one has offered it, and if they did,
I would not have taken it,
For I knew no love.
You can't recognize love
If you've never had it,
And so you can't receive it
If you don't know it's there.
So how do you know
If you've fallen in love,
When you've had no love?
And how do you know,
If you think you've fallen in
   love,
What it means when you fall in
   love,
If love has never been inside
   you?

He's Born...
I keep seeing the color red. It's warm. She must have had red on her hands when she held him, for he is warm, and she loves him. And her lips would be red too. —SA

Soliloquy

Ah. But today...
Today I met someone,
And I think I'm falling in love.
It makes no sense,
Because I don't know love,
Yet love is what I think I feel.
It happened so fast,
So much a blur before my eyes,
Such a surprise,
So unexpected.
I wouldn't know if it's love,
Not for sure,
But it feels like I think love might feel,
If I were ever to have felt it.
What I feel must be
Not because of me, but because
His love is very strong,
And it took me over.
That must be why I feel what I feel,
If what I feel is love.

He seems to know me
Like he's always known me,
   Like a stirring in my soul
Because I've found The One
That I want to be with forever.
The stirring is because
Of how he treated me
When we first met.
He didn't shy away from me
Because of how I look,
Or because of what I've done,
Or because of where I've been.
He knew all about me, about everything
But it didn't stop him.
He just came right at me
As though I were beautiful
And took my heart in his hands
And held it near him
And made it warm
And soft.

He Dies...
The red continues, and
exudes from him,
forever it seems;
always giving, always
forgiving. —JA

This must be love,
For what else could it be?
It isn't harsh,
Or harmful,
Or terrible,
Or terrorizing.
It doesn't want to destroy me,
Or take advantage of me.
I know all about that.
I've had enough of that.
This isn't that.
This feels the opposite.

So maybe that's how I'll know?
I'll know it's love because it doesn't make me
Want to hurt myself?
Because it makes me feel good—and—real?
And if I'm right,
And if it's love,
Now what?
It's been a whole day
And he hasn't left me.
No one has ever stuck with me *that*
   long before.
Does that mean this love
Will last forever?
How long is forever?
Will there ever be anything I could do
Or anything he doesn't know
About me
That he might find out
About me
That would make him
Leave me?

I want to know what love means,
To know what happens
When you fall in love.
To know
If life will be different,

If I'll be happy, and satisfied.
To know
If there's a good future.
To see,
For a change.
Maybe it all depends
Upon who
You love,
And who
Loves you.
If this is The One
I've been looking for,
If it's really love,
Then maybe he will help me
Help me to find out
What love is all about.

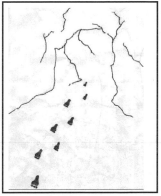

He Lives...
His footprints would be
red the day he left the
tomb, because the red
helps you remember. —SA

glossary

Ancient/Future—I'm not certain where this phrase originated, though I became acquainted with it from reading Leonard Sweet's book, *SoulTsunami* (Grand Rapids: Zondervan, 1999). It is the strange phenomenon of the connection between what is very old (if not ancient) and what is now. In other words, what is ancient is also future. Ancient rituals and practices are recurring in daily life and in worship, with current meaning and future direction.

Christendom—The many years in which Christianity was the dominant religion in the United States. During this time, Christianity was referenced in textbooks, television, government, and other avenues of life. In postmodernity, Christendom is dead.

Cultural manifestations—The phenomenon of God revealing himself through our worship of him and in the culture.

DNA—In churches, DNA is the church's God-given identity regarding mission and calling. DNA in churches includes mission, vision, values, and beliefs.

EBA—Easum, Bandy & Associates. For more information, check out the Web site <www.easumbandy.com>.

Experiential worship—Worship that values "experiencing" Jesus over "learning" about Jesus. It includes multimedia, multisensory, presentation, and participation. There are many different experiences of Jesus.

Genetic code—The church's DNA.

"Mechanical" metaphor—A way of describing the structure that supports Christendom churches. A mechanically structured church would thrive on "being fixed," or repaired. The mechanical metaphor helps illustrate how easy it is for Christendom churches and church leaders to be more concerned about the "mechanics" of the organization and making sure there is a "smooth" operation, than about the people who are in that organization. Mechanical churches are often "committee" structured.

Modern era—I recently asked Brian McLaren to offer a definition of the modern era.[1] He said, "Modernity refers to the era following the Middle Ages, an era characterized by (a) rising confidence in reason (epitomized by the Enlightenment), (b) increasing value placed on the individual (expressed in liberal democracy and consumerism), (c) the conquest of mystery and human limitations by science and technology, (d) expansion of Western European/American influence globally, and (e) a decrease in confidence in the church and religion." I gain the most insight into modernity when I compare it to postmodernity.

Multimedia—The mixture of media in worship. Examples include Microsoft PowerPoint, video, computer animation, and so on.

Multisensory—The focus on the five senses when planning and leading worship, by recognizing that God uses all the senses

---

1. Brian McLaren is a frequent speaker and writer on the topic of ministry and the current culture. Some of his books include *The Church on the Other Side: Doing Ministry in the Postmodern Matrix* (Grand Rapids: Zondervan, 2000); *Finding Faith: A Self-Discovery Guide for Your Spiritual Quest* (Grand Rapids: Zondervan, 1999); *A New Kind of Christian* (San Francisco: Jossey-Bass, 2001); *More Ready Than You Realize: Evangelism as Dance in the Postmodern Matrix* (Grand Rapids: Zondervan, 2002).

to reach a human heart. Multisensory worship includes not only electronic multimedia, but also live art, music, dance, or drama.

"Organic" metaphor—A way of describing churches that seem to be prospering in postmodernity. Organically oriented churches grow and nurture people, and don't focus on the structure, except as a way to fulfill a mission. In organically structured churches, the structure of an organism exists to allow freedom for the organism to blossom and fulfill its purpose. Organically structured organisms are "team" oriented.

Participative worship—Worship that encourages congregational involvement in singing, listening, ritual, and other activities.

Postmodernity—In a recent Internet forum on Ministry in the Postmodern Era for which Brian McLaren was the facilitator,[2] I learned from Brian that the term "postmodernity" was first used around 1950 "to describe approaches to architecture that were concerned with going beyond functionality, that tended to mix and match elements from architectural epochs, and that often incorporated whimsy into their designs." Postmodernity also became associated with "poststructuralism and deconstruction . . . movements in literary criticism that tried to emphasize the role of the READER (not just the writer) in the creation of a text." Observers began to note "some kind of harmonic resonance between, say, these new movements in literary criticism and several movements in philosophy, architecture, and even the new science (relativity, expanding universe, matter as energy, etc.)." Brian suggests that postmodernism "at its best" is seeking to "synthesize modernity and postmodernity."

---

2. Excerpts from Brian's forum post about "The Origin of Postmodernism" were taken from Easum, Bandy & Associates, The EBA Community, Coaching Seminars <www.easumbandy.com>. See the definition on the modern era to read more from and about Brian McLaren.

Pre-Christian—The person who doesn't yet know Jesus, who is similar to the person of two thousand years ago who didn't yet know Jesus. "Pre-Christian" is the profile of people in many segments of the population in the postmodern era.

Presentational worship—Worship that is more like a show and requires very little congregational participation, other than watching and listening.

acknowledgments

INTERVIEWS

I offer my thanks to the following churches and leaders who helped give me insight into the different shapes and sizes of teams in the local church.

Clark Crebar, founding pastor of Celebration, the Gen-X worship ministry of First Covenant Church of Sacramento, California.

Troy Dean, lead pastor (Minister of Changed Hearts) of University Praise in Fullerton, California.

Junius Dotson, founding pastor of Genesis, an African American congregation in the Silicon Valley of California.

Pam Fickensher, founder and lead pastor of Spirit Garage, a Gen-X ministry in downtown Minneapolis, Minnesota.

Josh Fox, worship minister of Graceland at Santa Cruz Bible Church in Santa Cruz, California.

Kristi Gaynor, minister of small groups at Hosanna! Lutheran Church in Lakeville, Minnesota.

Adam Hamilton, founding pastor of Church of the Resurrection in Kansas City, Kansas.

Michelle Hargrave, founding pastor of Praxis, a Gen X ministry in downtown Minneapolis, Minnesota.

Eric Herron, worship minister at New Song, in Covina, California.

Dave Householder, teaching pastor at Hosanna! Lutheran Church in Lakeville, Minnesota.

173

Dan Kimball, founding pastor of Graceland, the Gen-X ministry of Santa Cruz Bible Church in Santa Cruz, California.

Dave Olson, worship minister at Hosanna! Lutheran Church in Lakeville, Minnesota.

Frank Selveggio, lead pastor of New Song Church in Covina, California.

Many thanks to Kathy Brearly, Bill Tenny-Brittain, Gary Nims, and Paul Krentz for sharing their favorite Web sites (p. 32).

ARTISTS' ACKNOWLEDGMENTS

Opening Scene: Susan Says, "Let's Talk . . ."

p. 17: "Susan Self-Portrait" by Anysia Starr; Josh Lindquist, photographer. Reprinted with permission by Mudcastle <www.mudcastle.org>.

p. 18: "Night Lights" by Todd Townley. Used by permission.

p. 18: "Occult Moon" by Cathy Townley.

pp. 19-20: Stained Glass Banners by Sue Kemnitz, "Communications Designer," DeSign Studios, Inc. <www.designsbysbk.com>. "All the glory goes to the master creator...my art is but a small reflection of the wonder of his creation around us."

Closing Scene: Soliloquy: What Does It Mean When You Fall in Love?

pp. 164-65, 167: "Susan's drawings" rendered by Todd Townley. Used by permission.